pure style
outside

pure style outside

Jane Cumberbatch
with photography by **Pia Tryde**

RYLAND
PETERS
& SMALL
LONDON NEW YORK

First published in the United Kingdom in 1998.
This compact version published in 2005
by Ryland Peters & Small
20–21 Jockey's Fields, London WC1R 4BW

ISBN: 1 84172 909 4

A CIP catalogue record for this book is available from
the British Library.

Printed and bound in China.

For this edition:
Designer **Luana Gobbo**
Senior editor **Annabel Morgan**
Picture research **Emily Westlake**
Production **Sheila Smith**
Art director **Gabriella Le Grazie**
Publishing director **Alison Starling**
Stylist **Jane Cumberbatch**
Assistant stylist **Fiona Craig-McFeely**
Assistant stylist **Alice Douglas**

www.rylandpeters.com

contents

INTRODUCTION

Pure Style Outside is about making the best of your outside space, no matter how small. It's about being practical and looking at resourceful solutions for making your outside area as colourful, sensuous and pleasing to be in as any room inside your home. *Pure Style Outside* is about colour: the shades that appear in nature – sky blues, rose pinks, sunflower yellows and cabbage greens, and decorative ideas that work well with these natural elements: white cotton canvas, trellis painted minty green or terracotta coloured walls. It looks at the textures that work together to make the outside a living, organic space, such as peeling paintwork, rusting metal furniture, weathered flowerpots and worn paving stones. *Pure Style Outside* is about adopting vernacular styles for everything from fencing to garden tools. There are ideas for planting rows of dahlias, climbing roses, clematis and morning glory, towering foxgloves and delphiniums, pots or beds of herbs and other edible produce. *Pure Style Outside* is about experiencing the simple pleasures in life – eating home-grown tomatoes fresh from the vine, cutting your own roses and the sheer peace of sitting outside on a warm starry night. It focuses on the decorative aspects of open-air living, and it is full of inspiring ideas for durable fabrics, simple garden furniture, and basic, good-looking tableware. Lastly, *Pure Style Outside* shows you how to appreciate the many sensuous qualities of the natural world – water, light and shade, scent and texture.

elements

Bring life to your outside space with a diversity of organic textures and colour. Take a simple but practical approach, and invest in hardwearing old-fashioned tools that do the job properly. Consider and take inspiration from the vernacular styles for decorative and functional detailing. Select colourful easy-to-grow flowers, and use fabrics and furniture to make your outside area a truly luxurious place.

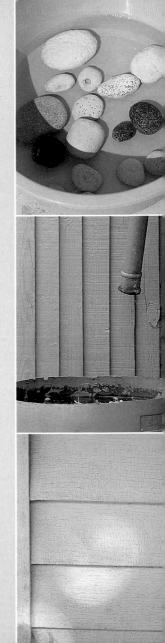

Colour

Colours change endlessly according to the seasons, the weather and the time of day. Strong sunlight on white walls dazzles the eyes with a harshness that makes us reach for a pair of sunglasses, whereas a dull day actually intensifies colours so they appear to leap out of the greyness. Consider colour in every aspect of outside living: plants, architectural details, furniture, fabrics and food. There is beauty in the simplest elements: a climbing white rose; green peas and beans growing in a vegetable patch; and a shady table laid with a crisp white cloth and bowls of green salad. Simple colour schemes for plants look distinctive, such as rows of brilliant-yellow sunflowers; a white wall covered with tumbling tendrils of sky-blue morning glory; or a window box painted pale green and planted with hedges of dwarf lavender. Enhance a sense of greenery by painting doors and windows in garden greens. Take note of vernacular styles, such as the colours of blinds and shutters in Mediterranean villages, or the shades of green paint that decorate sheds and fences in old-fashioned allotments. Make your outside space more of a room with colourful cushions and awnings: try classic shades of white or blue, or bold combinations like vivid orange and pink.

whitewash

stone

canvas

pebble

WHITE

The simplicity of white makes it a purist's dream colour and a versatile tool: white flowers can be used as a foil for greenery and white garden accessories look crisp. Although I am tempted to grow flowers in all my favourite colours, I stick to mainly white as ultimately it is the look most soothing to the urban eye. Each spring I look forward to the sweet-smelling white flowers that bloom on the climbing *Rosa* 'Madame Alfred Carrière', an old-fashioned rose that thrives in its shady environment. White *Clematis montana* produces hundreds of star-like flowers that spread in May along my roof-terrace railings. Perfect for shade is the less-rampant *C.* 'Henryi', which produces huge white flowers during the summer and has even bloomed in a warm December. Spiky foxgloves are good for height and attract bees, but most are biennial. For smart, almost instant window-box material I buy pots of white asters, available in early summer. Bright whitewashed walls are typical of sun-drenched Mediterranean patios and the look is easy to create with white exterior paint. I use white emulsion to transform everything from flowerpots to trellis; when it looks grubby or worn I simply repaint it, although old chairs and tables with blistered, peeling paint can look charming. White cushions and cloths look wonderful outside and create an airy, summery feel. I use old sheets for tablecloths and prewashed canvas for cushions and awnings, so the whole lot can be revived in the wash.

BLUE

Blue, the colour of the sea and sky, and flowers like bluebells, agapanthus and delphiniums, combines well with pink, white or yellow. As a single colour it looks dramatic: a wall covered with morning glory blooms, a fence bordered with cornflowers, or a bank of irises. Sheds, window boxes and pots look jaunty painted in bright, breezy shades. Look to the Aegean for inspiration and create a rich sea blue by mixing a few drops of blue universal stainer into a can of white emulsion. A whitewashed patio looks fabulous with blue and white cotton cushions and tablecloths, while practical, inexpensive blue plastic cloths and plates look cheery.

Cloud

Bluebell

Sea

Berry

Bean

Fig

Mint

Shed

GREEN

The array of greens in a vegetable patch illustrates the vast spectrum of shades: purplish green cabbages, lime-green lettuces and glossy peas packed in their pods. However commonplace, there is beauty in silvery green lavender, shiny rosemary, lime-green alchemilla and even a stretch of lush lawn. In spring, young leaves are luminous and bright with a yellow hue, and as the season progresses they darken to richer shades of green. Potting-shed greens are the shades devised by generations of gardeners who have painted fences, sheds, doors and seats in basic colours from ironmongers – these are useful in blending unobtrusively with their surroundings, and also create an illusion of greenery when foliage is sparse. Sea green or mint are more modern and have a Mediterranean feel; they look smart against galvanized metal buckets and pink and lavender-coloured flowers. Green-and-white striped canvas is useful for deck chairs and awnings, and is the sort of utilitarian material that is still found in traditional ironmongers.

PINK

Pink is a classic garden colour, and photographs of glorious pink and lavender borders of delphiniums, foxgloves, roses, sweet peas and peonies are what we hanker after and pore over in glossy garden books – the images would be complete with ourselves in appropriate gardening attire (a big floppy straw sun hat, with secateurs and an old trug). Nature has so exquisitely matched pink with green: think of spiky lavender heads on silvery green stems, or fuchsia-pink foxglove bells on lime-green stalks. I love to see trellis with pink rambling roses, or a garden wall flanked by towering pink hollyhocks. Fluffy allium balls are good for creating height, and clusters of pinks are pretty edging borders. Pink is a fabulous colour for summer table settings. I have a cloth and chair covers in an old Laura Ashley cotton Provençal print which look particularly vibrant. Pink-and-orange checked napkins will enliven a plain white cloth, and deep fuchsia place mats look great with lime-green napkins and jugs of pink roses and alchemilla. To complete the effect, serve tasty pink puddings like raspberry jelly embedded with fruit or home-made strawberry ice-cream.

Hollyhock

Sweet pea

Allium

Pansy

ORANGE

Garish and regimented municipal-park displays have made orange flowers unpopular with modern gardeners, and although splashes of orange would be unwelcome in a classic pink, lavender and white country-garden border, it is a wonderful, daring hot colour that can add vibrancy and spice to an outside space. Borders of marigolds in a vegetable garden look pleasing and deter caterpillars and snails, while pots of tall orange lilies look good on a balcony or terrace. Orange and pink are an exciting combination – try modern hybrid orange roses with old-fashioned pinks and cerises, and there are rich orange and pink varieties in the dahlia family, until recently considered rather kitsch. Dahlias are beautiful, but need to be grown in an orderly fashion, say, as part of a vegetable plot. The cut flowers look wonderful in a simple jam jar. I vowed not to have any orange in my almost-white garden, but couldn't resist packs of nasturtium seeds. They are foolproof to plant in pots and will trail up a wigwam of sticks producing endless orange, yellow and scarlet flowers. There is something inviting and luxuriant about the neat avenues of trees laden with jewel-like oranges in southern Europe. A bowl of fat oranges with their leaves still attached makes a wonderful table decoration, and white jugs stuffed with marigolds also create vibrant splashes of colour on a white tablecloth.

Earth

Tomato

Pumpkin

Terracotta

YELLOW

Reassuring bursts of yellow daffodils, narcissi
and tulips punctuate city gardens and the
countryside in spring, confirming that all the
colour hasn't drained away during the winter. I
like to plant pots, tubs and window boxes
outside the kitchen with dwarf daffodils and
narcissi, which have a wonderful heady scent.
As a child I used to plant daffodil bulbs and
keep them hidden away in a cupboard until
spring; it was sheer magic to watch the shoots
grow and produce a mass of yellow trumpets. I
also have a fascination for sunflowers and
cannot believe they can grow quite so tall and
produce such giant glowing heads in so few
weeks. Try planting rows of sunflowers to
make a natural border or to create shelter from
the wind. Other yellow favourites include
honeysuckle, which is easy to grow from
cuttings and has a glorious scent that
intensifies during the evening, and pretty pale
hollyhocks flanking a front door. For the
outside table, yellow and green make a stylish
combination, and a yellow-and-white checked
tablecloth and napkins look cheery and bright,
bringing a dash of sunshine to the garden. Grill
courgettes and decorate them with edible
courgette flowers – wildly expensive in smart
greengrocers but virtually free if you grow your
own. For pudding, I serve creamy yellow
peaches in simple butter-yellow pottery bowls.

Candle

Honeysuckle

Nasturtium

Hay

Surfaces and structures

Organic, natural and synthetic surfaces combine to make the garden a living, breathing space. Nature creates an ever-changing textural picture: consider dry, sun-baked terracotta and the same surface after a heavy storm, darkened and glistening. Many surfaces improve with age and exposure to the elements, such as sun-blistered peeling paint on an old garden table, the bleached silvery grey of a weathered oak chair, or an irregular hand-thrown terracotta pot, crumbling with moss and age. For boundaries there are diverse materials such as old red brickwork, New England-style feather-boarding, and simple wood-and-wire or stick fencing. For underfoot, old red-brick pavers can be laid in a herringbone pattern to edge borders or make a pathway in a vegetable plot. Smooth square terracotta tiles look distinctive laid in a checquerboard pattern, and a line of old worn York flagstones creates a simple, useful path. Alternatively, there are cobbles, gravel and luxurious soft lawn. Water is a sensuous, cooling surface, and merely filling up an old sink or bucket lined with pebbles and shells creates a simple makeshift pool. Textural fabrics for outdoor use include canvas for awnings and woven cane or rattan for seating.

TEXTURE

Contrasting textures in the garden are surprising and exciting, with tactile elements like rough weatherboarding, blistering paint, balls of hairy string – useful for a multitude of gardening jobs – and besom brooms with twiggy bristles. The feel of a rough weathered flowerpot or a bleached wooden trug together with the smooth coolness of metal tools make any garden task a sensuous experience. After pounding city streets, treat tired feet to a soft, springy lawn, or a carpet of scented thyme or camomile. It is satisfying to march down a crunchy gravel path or sunbathe on worn York flagstones, while teak decking, a good material for a pool-side area or terrace, feels smooth to the touch. Coarse canvas is a natural, practical fabric for seat covers and awnings, and acts as a foil to indulgent feather-filled cushions and soft throws used for siestas. There are also the textures of a dry garden, which contrast with those of damp soil and dripping plants, newly watered or after a storm, when leaves are bent double by jewel-like drops of water.

UNDERFOOT SURFACES

Deciding what lies underfoot in your garden space is important in both practical and visual terms. The courtyard at the back of my house is laid with old brick pavers that were found ten years ago in a salvage yard. They are a rich red terracotta, which has weathered enough to look as if they were laid when the house was built nearly 300 years ago. Old creamy yellow York flagstones were another option that I considered, but they were more costly to transport and to lay. Garden paths create a sense of order and lead the eye in exciting, sometimes unexpected directions. A diminutive flower and vegetable garden that I know in America's Catskill Mountains is criss-crossed by a series of swept hard-earth pathways, an idea transplanted from the southern states where the owner grew up. An enclosed herb and vegetable garden in Connecticut is more formally bisected by uneven brick avenues, while a London allotment belonging to a friend of mine is divided by irregularly shaped slabs of stone. Smooth terracotta tiles laid in simple geometric chequerboard patterns are perfect for hot Mediterranean patios as they retain heat and are delicious to walk on barefoot in the cool of the evening. They can be obtained quite cheaply from builder's merchants in France, Spain and Italy, or from local suppliers who import them. It is also worth looking out for tiles salvaged from old farmhouses. The irregularity of rough, uneven cobbled surfaces is appealing, and I am inspired by the marble-chip patios, pavements and alleyways found in many Spanish villages. Other aggregates, such as gravel, create textural, crunchy paths that are practical and reasonably maintenance-free. Specialized suppliers will provide everything from white marble cobblestones and green marble pebbles, to beach pebbles, cockleshells and terracotta shingle. Teak or pine decking has a seaside look inspired by boardwalks at the beach and is a useful surface for roof gardens or small terraces where heavier materials are not suitable. For a greener, softer garden surface, the obvious choice is a velvety lawn. More unusual are flagstones with herbs like camomile or thyme planted between the cracks, which emanate a delicious scent when crushed underfoot.

BOUNDARIES

The earliest gardens were contained for practical reasons – for privacy, to exclude vermin and simply to enclose a cultivated area of ground. As well as protecting plants from frost, walled gardens feel secretive and romantic. Gather ideas from vernacular styles for fences and walls when choosing a boundary for your garden or vegetable patch: New England linear picket fencing is charming, and flat plank fencing can be painted or left unfinished to weather and bleach. Improvised fences of sticks or pieces of curved wattle look rustic and decorative in small vegetable gardens, while a row of espaliered fruit trees or pleached limes and neatly clipped box hedges create natural, green boundaries. To create decorative borders for beds, try rows of smooth, round pebbles, lengths of bent or woven wattle, or scalloped Victorian terracotta tiles. Another boundary that should not be overlooked is the facade of the house. Even if the only outside space you have is a window box, think about the colour and texture of the

wall around it. A white-painted box planted with white daisies and set against white featherboarding evokes a simple New England cottage, while white-washed walls create a Mediterranean feel and are ideal for small patios as they reflect light and enhance the sense of space. Roses and honeysuckle look pretty trained up the facade of a brick house, or the flat features of modern walling can be alleviated with paint. The rich barn red that wooden cabins and sheds are painted all over North America and Scandinavia makes a good backdrop for plants and furniture. I mixed up a greenish blue shade for a stretch of new wall, and this also makes a perfect ground for plants or topiary box trees in metal buckets.

SHEDS

On a train journey to any large English city you see patchworks of allotment gardens, the plots often sandwiched between bus depots and electricity pylons. The allotment holders are a mixture of knowledgeable old-timers and a younger generation of gardeners who want their children to know that vegetables come from the earth, rather than from cellophane packs. Everyone has a shed, no matter how makeshift or eccentric, and a look inside any might reveal deck chairs; string; raffia; yoghurt pots for seedlings; and an array of tools. Vegetable patches and allotment-style gardens need year-round attention, from spring when bulbs begin flowering and the soil is hoed and fertilized in preparation for planting, through summer when fruits and vegetables ripen, weeds are battled with and watering is a constant activity, to autumn when plants are cut back and produce is harvested. These gardens require soil that is fertile, well drained, well tilled and weed free. Light, crumbly soil allows air to enter, which sustains the organisms that make up healthy earth, if soil is hard when dry, and sticky when wet, dig in as much organic material as you can to lighten it. With increased popularity in organic growing methods, many gardeners are keen to make their own compost. If you have space, a compost heap is essential, with ingredients such as tea bags, eggshells, vegetable peelings, manure and grass cuttings. Keep it moist with water and turn the heap occasionally to aerate it. If you have restricted growing space, you will probably need to resort to manufactured fertilizers. I buy bone meal and apply a weekly dose of Miracle Grow to help my roses, delphiniums, foxgloves, clematis, herbs, lettuces and tomatoes. I also apply horse manure in early summer and autumn.

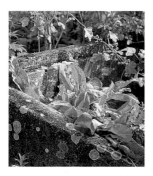

ARBOURS, ARCHES AND PERGOLAS

There is a fashion for growing anything from nasturtiums and tomatoes to runner beans and sweet peas up wigwam shapes made of canes or twigs. The effect is decorative, easy to achieve, and a practical way of training plants. Single sticks of wood set in serried rows are another functional but charming way of training beans and other climbers that do not produce heavy fruits, and 'hedges' of thin twiggy sticks are great for training sweet peas. For really simple but effective structures, buy lengths of chicken wire from hardware shops. Alternatively, simple wooden square trellis looks smart painted a shade of garden green: I used it for training clematis over an ugly stretch of wall on my roof garden. Arbours, arches and pergolas create shady areas in which to relax, and are also decorative ways of supporting roses and other flowers. Metal rose arches can be obtained from garden centres or mail-order catalogues; the rather unsightly finish that many come in can be concealed with tough enamel paint. Twiggy pergolas made of sticks are romantic and easy to construct, but coat the ends that sit in the earth with an anti-rot preparation. A shady vine pergola is like a little outside room, and can be made by training a grapevine or other vigorous climber over a wooden or wire-and-metal structure.

Containers

Almost anything will do as a plant container: plastic bowls, old sinks, terracotta pots, wooden tubs and galvanized metal buckets are just some examples. Containers make focal points within a garden and can be moved whenever you feel like it. Try a pair of tubs with standard box or bay trees on either side of a door, or mass together terracotta pots filled with herbs. Create a miniature garden on a windowsill or balcony with window boxes containing anything from little lavender hedges to trailing nasturtiums, vegetables or herbs. Wooden seed trays, picket-fence window boxes and twiggy troughs are all useful for displaying pots of herbs, spring bulbs and summer bedding plants. For added colour I paint pots in shades of green, blue or white. Good drainage is the key to success, and normal-size pots with a central hole need only a few stones in the bottom before being filled with soil. For a well-balanced potting medium, use soil that is light, friable, easily drained and nourishing. Mix heavy soil with sharp river sand, and light soil with rich loam. Add granulated peat to help retain moisture, and fertilizer to provide nourishment. With the addition of compost and regular feeding, potted plants will remain healthy in the same soil for many years.

TERRACOTTA

Shapes range from traditional potting-shed flowerpots to giant Ali-Baba urns. Good garden specialists import wonderful textural terracotta pots from Spain, Italy, France and Morocco. Salvage and reclamation yards are good sources of old hand-thrown flowerpots. Machine-made terracotta pots look uniform and lack the texture and irregularities of hand-thrown examples. To add instant character to cheap pots I mix up a wash of white emulsion coloured with green, blue or terracotta. Pots left out in the elements weather quite quickly, but you can accelerate the process by smearing them with yoghurt to encourage green moss to grow. I use giant terracotta pots in all shapes for planting clematis, tomatoes, honeysuckle and lavender, and rectangular containers placed against a wall for growing taller things like foxgloves and delphiniums. Create a windowsill or balcony kitchen garden with herbs in individual pots: rosemary, parsley, mint, marjoram, rocket, sage, thyme and basil grow well with a strict daily watering regime. Or use terracotta pots for vegetables: I have attempted lettuces, trailing tomatoes and dwarf cherry tomatoes with success. For a structured look, round box balls look architectural in square terracotta pots, while little box or bay standards suit pots with a round shape.

BELOW *Ideal for a rooftop or balcony vegetable garden is a long tom flowerpot painted in vibrant lime-green emulsion with a wigwam of pea sticks and raffia to support a cherry tomato plant.*

LEFT *Old terracotta bowls look decorative planted with herbs or bedding plants like pansies, but make sure there is a hole for drainage.*

RIGHT *A pot painted lime-green and planted with an ornamental cabbage looks good on a windowsill or terrace wall.*

BELOW *A terracotta rhubarb forcer can either be planted with tiny trailing flowers or left empty as a decorative feature.*

BELOW *A shallow planter filled with low-growing mind-your-own-business.*

BELOW, LEFT TO RIGHT *Pansies in a pot that's been white-washed for a weathered effect; two terracotta tom pots planted with amaryllis and a topiary box tree.*

RIGHT *An old powder-blue enamelled camping dish is an idea for planting violas and other tiny flowering plants.*

ABOVE *Ornamental curly kale cabbages in a simple galvanized metal container make an unusual decoration for the table or windowsill.*

RIGHT *A basic metal tin is ideal for growing wheat grass – an organic wonder root that can be liquidized to make a nourishing drink.*

RIGHT *The silvery green leaves and rough texture of aromatic lavender work successfully with metal containers such as this florist's display bucket.*

RIGHT *A weathered metal bucket is a no-nonsense, yet very pleasing, container for a box standard.*

OPPOSITE *A shapely bay standard in a metal bucket can be placed on a table outdoors to create a sense of height.*

METAL

Functional and simple metal kit for the garden, such as galvanized metal watering cans and dustbins, and corrugated-iron shacks and sheds have a rough, honest appeal and create a foil to the softness of plants and flowers. Metal plant containers – whether they are buckets, troughs, bowls or old cans – have a tough, utilitarian feel, and their modern look makes a refreshing change from traditional stone or terracotta containers. The silvery grey colour of the metal works well with greenery, and the textured galvanized surfaces look good contrasted with silvery grey-green lavender leaves or shiny dark-green rosemary bushes. Simple architectural shapes such as topiary box or bay look smart and stylish in metal buckets, which can be bought for just a few pounds from hardware shops. You can even recycle baked-bean or tomato tins and make them into vases for cut flowers or, with small holes punched in the bottom for drainage, containers for herbs.

WOOD & PLASTIC

For a rustic look, a basic rectangular window box in a strong hardwood like cedar can be left to weather a lovely silvery grey or painted to unify with doors, walls and furniture. It is such fun to pick your own juicy tomatoes and to have a few herbs at hand for giving delicious flavour to suppers of fish, new potatoes and salad. A simple window-box kitchen garden could have herbs like chives and parsley at the back and trailing cherry tomatoes at the front. Or, for a simple, uniform scheme, plant white or blue hyacinths, hedges of dwarf lavender, nasturtiums or white asters. Wooden slatted tubs, barrel shaped or square, can be filled with anything from wild flowers and herbs to topiary box trees or giant sunflowers. Wooden seed trays, filled with pots of herbs, look good displayed on outdoor tables. Steer clear of plastic pots and window boxes in soulless colours and shapes. Be inventive and adapt brightly coloured washing-up bowls and buckets, in vivid greens and blues, from a hardware or discount shop, for a more contemporary look.

LEFT *Basic and traditional wooden seed trays are a practical and innovative way of displaying pots of flowers or herbs.*

ABOVE *Sky-blue and sea-green plastic pots are an alternative to terracotta. Use as a table decoration or display several on a sill.*

BELOW *For a plain, natural effect, fill an unpainted junk box with silvery thyme and rosemary.*

ABOVE LEFT *An old wooden box has been given a face-lift with coats of white emulsion to make a simple window box for flowers or herbs.*

ABOVE RIGHT *Based on the design of egg boxes, these* functional cardboard seed trays are available from any good garden centre.

BELOW *Plain white, inexpensive plastic cups make useful and simple pots for planting young plants and seedlings.*

BOTTOM LEFT *An ugly plastic window box has been transformed with two coats of powder-blue emulsion, then planted with ornamental kale cabbages for a contemporary look.*

BOTTOM RIGHT *A window box with picket-fence detail, filled with a selection of herbs in small white pots, makes an attractive kitchen garden where little space is available.*

Plants

It is exciting to grow your own flowers, herbs and fruits – and you do not have to be an expert to be successful at it. It is just as pleasing to nurture a window box or grow rocket from seed as it is to plan a large-scale garden. Colour is the most important criterion for me when it comes to choosing plants. My favourites remind me of childhood summers: white climbing roses; fat purple alliums; white and pink-purple clematis; pink foxgloves; deep-blue and lavender delphiniums; blowsy pink peonies; and gaudy orange, pink, white and red dahlias. I am an impatient gardener who wants the picture on the seed packet to be realised overnight. It is satisfying to take a cutting of a plant like honeysuckle, stick it in the earth, and actually see it start to shoot a few days later. Yet with the constraints of domestic hurly-burly, it is more sensible to invest in pots of young plants from reputable garden centres. When it comes to homegrown produce, it is possible to grow things in surprisingly confined spaces: I had a good crop of tomatoes this summer from four or five plants in pots on the roof garden, plus nasturtiums and rocket grown from seed. There are also pots of herbs that grow well — basil, mint, thyme, and rosemary — just some essentials to have for flavouring everything from fish to salads.

FLOWERS

I am not a serious gardener since colour is my main priority when choosing flowers. I am not concerned with planting fashionable varieties and I probably make dreadful gardening gaffes simply because I want the colours to look right together. I am sure it is not de rigueur to mix tomatoes, nasturtiums and white clematis – a group I had on my roof terrace – but against the dreary urban roof-scape of concrete and brick, the bursts of vibrant orange, yellow, scarlet and white on a backdrop of greenery looked cheery. My dream is for a totally white garden (much like my ideal white minimalist interior), scented, romantic and flowering all year. To achieve the former I need a lot more gardening expertise than I am prepared to gain, and with three children the interior vision is not meant to be – at least for a few years. Therefore, I am content to be less exacting about colour in the garden and to experiment and make mistakes. I stick loosely to a palette of individual colours that also marry well with each other: white, pink, lavender, and hot oranges and yellows. I find that blocks of single colours tend to be more dramatic and less confusing to the eye, like a wall smothered with white roses, tubs of green topiary box standards, or a path edged with pinks. For height and drama I love foxgloves, especially white ones. Having disdained this woodland plant for years as a self-seeding weed,

OPPOSITE, CLOCKWISE FROM TOP LEFT Agapanthus, with ball-like flowers on slim green stems; passion flowers, which are vigorous climbers; delicate white violas; pretty blue border geraniums; foxgloves – easy to grow, but most are biennial; delicate lavender poppies.

BELOW Pretty blue and mauve delphiniums are excellent for adding height to a border and are easy to grow.

gardeners now compete to produce varieties for flower shows in the most subtle shades of pink, white and lavender. The tag that came with my appropriately named 'Albino' describes the majestic spikes of tubular white flowers that bloom during June and July, and, of course, the warning that foxgloves are toxic if eaten. I managed to grow them in large pots on the roof with quite satisfactory results. One day I will plant pots of white agapanthus, whose graceful stems support lacy heads – another good plant for height that grows well in sunny spots. Delphiniums seem ridiculously easy for amateurs like me to grow and their tall spikes with a froth of blue and mauve flowers exist quite happily in potting composts enriched regularly with bone meal and plant food. Climbing white roses and pot-grown rambling clematis are other favourites that are good for camouflaging unsightly objects. Passion flower is a pretty climber that grows well in sheltered positions. The blooms only last a day or so, but are produced so freely that there is a constant display from June to September, often followed by edible bright-orange fruit. Morning glory is another eager half-hardy annual that produces myriad trumpet-shaped flowers, in sky blue, magenta or deep pink, from June to September. The flowers last only part of a day, normally closing during early afternoon, but, shaded from the midday sun, they may last until evening. A traditional cottage-garden flower with late-

OPPOSITE, TOP AND BOTTOM *Peonies look beautiful even after heavy rain; morning glory's trumpet flowers live less than 24 hours.*

CLOCKWISE, FROM TOP LEFT *Poppies look wonderful in wild, uncut grass; border geraniums add a touch of delicacy; foxgloves look good in rural and urban gardens; voluptuous, rain-soaked summer roses.*

summer blooms, often used to edge a path or potato patch, the perennial dahlia is ideally suited to making a brash colour statement. With many varieties and glorious combinations of white, crimson, pink, yellow and purple – some with two colours in one stem – dahlias are making a comeback in gardening circles. Zinnias are another showy flower in gorgeous orange and pink, with broad and flat, rolled, or even frilled petals. They flower in late summer and give life to a border. While carnations are deemed rather kitsch, the common garden pink, which is in the same family, is a pretty, feathery, old-fashioned border flower, which is easy to grow and maintain.

OPPOSITE, CLOCKWISE FROM TOP LEFT *Dahlias make bold colour statements; a fuchsia-pink dog rose; a feathery petalled dahlia; colourful home-grown nasturtiums; a vibrant zinnia.*

BELOW, LEFT AND RIGHT *Poppies growing in long grass; pretty cottage-garden pinks.*

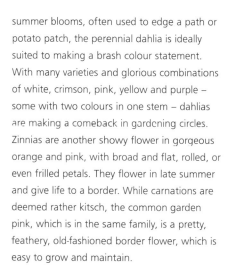

HERBS

Herbs look beautiful and taste good: chamomile or thyme are fragrant planted between flagstones; parsley, thyme and mint make good cottage-garden beds; and rosemary or bay can be clipped into architectural shapes. Even if you are restricted to a windowsill or balcony, it is possible to grow in containers most of the herbs needed for cooking. Tomato salads and sauces without basil would be dull, and I generally keep a plant in the warmest, most sheltered spot for the duration of summer and freeze sprigs for use in winter. Sage grows quite happily on the roof terrace and is reasonably hardy. I love the strongly scented leaves chopped sparingly into sauces and salads. Part of the pleasure of growing rosemary is cutting the spikes, which releases the heavenly sharp scent. Used sparingly, rosemary is delicious with pork, chicken and roasted vegetables. Mint has an irresistible smell and flavour, and grows like wildfire. I use tiny sprigs to decorate ice cream and to add flavour to new potatoes. Lemon balm is useful to add to wine punches and salads and it is a pleasure to pinch the scented leaves and enjoy the aromas that are released.

BOTTOM, LEFT AND RIGHT *Sage keeps its leaves throughout the winter and tastes good in stuffing and stews; basil, delicious in salads and sauces, thrives in sheltered spots but is destroyed by the first hint of frost.*

OPPOSITE, CLOCKWISE FROM TOP LEFT *Parsley is a versatile herb that is good in salads; lavender looks and smells great and can be used to flavour biscuits; lemon balm grows vigorously and is delicious in punches; drought-resistant rosemary is deliciously aromatic.*

PRODUCE

I have always had a fascination for seed packets and the magnificent specimens that are promised in the illustrations. Even though we lived in London with little room for a vegetable patch, my parents grew courgettes, tomatoes and raspberries covered in bridal-like veiling to keep off the birds. We had two big plum trees, one a Victoria that bent double and eventually collapsed with its yield of fat, juicy plums. My mother was endlessly making jam and there always came a point when my sister and I never wanted to see a plum again. My family and I are learning to grow things using the knowledge of the villagers near our house in Spain. We have learnt how to plant, stake and care for tomatoes, how to dip ridges for potatoes, how to take the seeds out of sunflowers and even how to thresh chickpeas. To cope with a glut of tomatoes, we skin and bottle them to store away for use in the winter in salads and stews. Even though the slugs and some kind of wilt threatened, we cut and ate our own magnificent cabbages which, lightly steamed with butter, even the under-eights ate without dissent. At home in England, apple trees provide fruit for cooking and eating, and there are plenty of strawberries, raspberries and gooseberries for delicious fools and jams. I have even been successful on my roof terrace this summer with a trailing variety of tomato that grew up wigwams of sticks and produced tasty rosy-red specimens. I have also had luck with rocket, which grows with ease from seed and is a delicious nutty and slightly bitter addition to salads. Wild food is especially fun to collect: blackberries come to mind immediately, and they make delicious jam and pies. Sloes, found in country hedgerows, are bitter raw, but they can be added to gin and left to steep for a few months to make a pink, sweet brew in time for Christmas.

Fabrics and furniture

Toughness and durability are essential qualities for outdoor fabrics and furniture. All-purpose cotton canvas works well for simple chair covers and shady awnings, while cream calico – cheap, durable and washable – is ideal for making tablecloths, loose covers and cushions. Another favourite understated fabric is blue-and-white ticking, a robust cotton twill closely woven in narrow stripes. Traditionally used for pillows and mattresses, it looks good in any setting, whether as cushions on a hot whitewashed patio, or as simple chair covers in a leafy garden. Plasticized cotton or PVC are useful for waterproof tablecloths and come by the metre from department stores. You don't have to invest in extra sets of furniture for outside: indoor foldable chairs can be whisked out when the sun shines, as can a lightweight table. If you prefer permanent outdoor furniture, hardwoods should be oiled regularly or coated with tough exterior paint. The alternative is the aged, weathered effect: peeling paint, algae-encrusted wood or rusty metal – organic textures that look at home with outside elements. There are plenty of outlets for junky furniture that can be left outside, but any expensive pieces should be brought inside once summer is over.

FABRICS

Fabrics need to be tough and hard-wearing for outside use. The best textures include canvas, linen and washable plastic. Department stores, haberdasheries and interior design shops are great sources of stripy deck-chair canvas, plasticized cottons for cloths and basic cotton calico. Heavy cotton canvas is one of the most adaptable fabrics and can be used to make sturdy loose covers for garden chairs. It is important to wash natural-fibre fabrics before cutting and sewing to prevent shrinkage later. I like to buy tough blue and white plain or striped cotton canvas to make awnings for my yard. The ends are hemmed and the corners punched with metal eyelets (very easy to do with a hole-punching kit). The awning is secured to hooks on the wall with nylon rope that can be adjusted as necessary. White and cream fabrics look fabulous, especially in a white-painted outside space. White cotton loose covers can disguise ill-matching chairs, and a white sheet flung over a table looks stylish. Scatter cushions should be filled with feathers and bench squabs should be of good-quality foam and have removable covers. Fabrics in vibrant seaside blues, apple greens and rosy pinks add colour and enhance surrounding flowers and greenery. Pink and orange cloths and napkins look bright and contemporary, while blue-and-white ticking for soft furnishings looks smart in any setting.

1

2

10

3

9

4

5

7

6

8

See page 140 for fabric details.

11

12

13

14

27

23

15

26

20

16

25

22

19

17

24

21

18

FURNITURE

Cheap, practical, but totally charmless, moulded plastic garden furniture has spread like a rash through parks, hotels and gardens. Here are some simple, decorative alternatives for seats and tables that combine form and function without breaking the bank. Anything that folds is useful, so it can be brought inside when the elements become inclement. My favourites are small folding slatted wooden tables spruced up with a lick of white emulsion each season. There are streamlined, contemporary folding chairs and loungers with lightweight aluminium frames and tough synthetic covers. Outside furniture can be very basic: a plain white cloth on a practical folding decorating table becomes stylish with a couple of jars of cut flowers and some white candles.

ABOVE *Simple wooden hardwood benches look good left in their natural state, or they can be painted, like this one in bright cornflower blue.*

RIGHT *This rocking deck chair folds away for easy storage. It has a light aluminium frame and a tough Textilene cover.*

ABOVE *Solid wooden garden tables are one of the most practical outdoor items. Painted surfaces weather well for an organic look.*

RIGHT *A vibrant checked cotton deck-chair cover is a zingy alternative to traditional stripes.*

RIGHT *Picked up in a junk shop, this old folding metal table looks good all year, and can be used to display pots of spring bulbs, or laid for summer meals.*

RIGHT *A white slatted folding chair with arms has a seaside look. Make it more comfy by adding cushions.*

ABOVE *A flat-pack pine potting bench has been updated with sea-blue emulsion. Use it to store flowerpots and tools, or as a table for food.*

RIGHT *A traditional deck chair in a tough blue-and-white checked cotton cover looks crisp and cheery in any outdoor setting.*

LEFT *Lightweight folding chairs are smart for outdoor dining. Old ones are often nicely worn and have rough, blistered paint.*

BELOW *This sun-lounger is made of aluminium with a Textilene all-weather seat. Ideal for camping, a sun deck, pool side or garden.*

BELOW, LEFT TO RIGHT *A folding decorator's table can be used for seating large groups of people. Smarten it up with a*

cloth. A director's chair, with a yellow checked cotton seat and back, is painted a sludgy gray to blend with greenery.

A small folding table is a good dining table for one. Put two or three together to accommodate larger numbers of people.

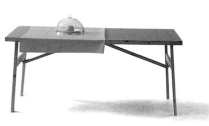

Accessories

Kitting out your outside space is no different from furnishing a room inside. The furniture will largely determine the look, so first decide whether to buy smart pieces that need to be stored inside during winter or to look around in junk shops for old metal or wooden tables, benches and chairs that can be left outside to weather and provide exterior detail all year round. A simple solution for outside eating is to buy a hardboard tabletop with separate trestles and folding chairs, which can be dressed up with natural fabrics like cotton, calico, canvas and ticking. There is enormous scope for creating stylish outside table settings. Forget the days when we were expected to lay dinner tables with immaculate sets of cutlery and cut-glass crystal. At the most basic level, unbreakable plastic cups, bowls and plates are useful for children and picnics, while simple white catering china, with enamelled tin bowls and jugs, creates a plain look that can be embellished with jugs of colourful flowers, glowing candles and napkins in brightly coloured checks. I have a passion for old glassware and love to mix odd glasses and jugs found in markets and junk shops. Whatever you choose, the only rule is to try to create informal settings that look wonderful, yet are simply achieved.

LIGHTING

Without doubt, the most sensuous outside lighting is candlelight at an alfresco supper or the flickering flames of a campfire. The only really pretty electric lights are white fairy lights, like those used on Christmas trees, which look magical strung in rows across a garden or patio. Cream candles are my favourite lights for outside and I have a store of empty jam jars which make really cheap but attractive containers. I also like glass storm lamps and find that a line of three or four along the table creates pools of soft light. Candles can be displayed effectively in basic metal lanterns from hardware shops, which are practical because they can be hung on hooks on the wall. For simple, cheap outdoor lighting buy bags of nightlights in metal holders. They look stylish in flickering groups of two dozen or so in the centre of a table or in lines along window ledges, or placed individually in niches in old walls. Nightlights can burn in a soft breeze but on windy evenings I put them in jam jars or old terracotta pots.

TOOLS

I have a few totally indispensable tools for my gardening activities, which live in the old coal cellar – my version of a potting shed. Most of my gardening is carried out in pots and window boxes, and my watering can is used twice a day in hot weather to satisfy the thirst of the potted plants. The essential fork, trowel and dibber are normally kept tucked into a pot, and secateurs and a pair of tough gloves are always at hand for pruning. There are also canes, wire and pieces of string for training new growth, and hats, old shirts and gumboots. I also keep cans of emulsion for painting trellis, pots and furniture, and plastic bottles of diluted washing-up liquid to rid the roses of greenfly and more potent insecticide to deal with blackfly that plague the nasturtiums.

RIGHT *Wooden-handled garden shears for trimming hedges and cutting back shrubs.*

LEFT *Keep a besom broom for sweeping up leaves and twigs, and a supply of cane pea sticks to build wigwams to train climbing plants.*

LEFT *A sturdy trowel is probably the most essential tool for a city gardener to plant window boxes and pots.*

ABOVE *Curvy and compact, traditional wooden trugs are shaped perfectly for carrying tools, plants and other gardening kit.*

ABOVE *A set of all-metal trowel, dibber and fork – essential tools for potting plants and seedlings – are practical and easy to clean.*

RIGHT AND BELOW *This plastic apron is practical gardening attire, together with a pair of tough gloves like these vinyl-coated ones.*

BELOW *A big plastic holdall like this is inexpensive and can be used to carry everything from picnic gear to logs from the wood shed.*

LEFT *I have several metal watering cans and this galvanized example is good because its boxy proportions make it easy to carry and pour.*

LEFT *Gumboots are the most sensible footwear for gardening jobs on soggy wet days – this pair is lined with leather for extra warmth.*

RIGHT *Bright-green refuse sacks are a jollier alternative to the ubiquitous black bin bags.*

RIGHT *A rake for leaves, a traditional pitchfork and a solid spade with a wooden handle are all useful implements for the gardener.*

ABOVE *Plant labels need not be boring to look at. Metal or wooden garden tags are much more stylish than plastic ones – and they are not expensive.*

ABOVE *Raffia and string are invaluable for all sorts of jobs, from tying tomato plants to canes, to hanging up bundles of bulbs to dry.*

UTENSILS

I use simple, basic, functional equipment and utensils for outdoor eating. Invaluable favourites include tough, unbreakable plastic bowls, plates and mugs, which can be bought really cheaply from hardware and chain stores. Tough glassware – such as anything made by Duralex – is not only practical, but looks very smart and is also widely available. For picnics and eating on the move I am very fond of my tiny metal barbecue, which gives out enough heat to cook a veritable feast of sausages, or delicious fresh fish, vegetables, and even bananas and marshmallows. Brewing up cups of steaming coffee on a Primus stove with a camping kettle is also a great way of keeping warm when picnicking on a sharp and clear winter's day.

LEFT *A tough white plastic salad bowl is practical in the garden.*

BELOW LEFT *Keep bottles cool with an insulated metal bottle cooler.*

BELOW RIGHT *This tray has been given a face-lift with blue emulsion.*

RIGHT *A simple galvanized metal jug, for serving glasses of ice-water or holding flowers, gives a robust, utilitarian look to outdoor table settings.*

FAR RIGHT *Reminiscent of those used in school dining rooms, a simple glass water jug looks good on an outside table, and is cheap and easy to find.*

ABOVE *If outdoor meals involve children, delicate cups and glasses are likely to end up in smithereens. Play safe with plastic mugs and sturdy Duralex glassware that comes in lots of smart shapes and even bounces when dropped.*

TOP LEFT *Enamelled tin plates and mugs are great camping basics and also look good at the table. You can find this utilitarian tableware in hardware stores and camping shops.*

TOP CENTRE *A traditional barbecue is good for cook-ups at home or on the beach. Although*

tiny, it will produce sufficient heat to cook four lamb cutlets followed by roast bananas in their skins.

TOP RIGHT *Department stores are good sources of cheap and cheerful, brightly coloured plastic tableware that is ideal for picnics and informal outside meals at home.*

LEFT *Napkins and place mats in bright solid colours or checks look best against plain cloths or bare wooden tabletops, and are cheerful even on the dullest summer's day.*

BELOW *For a luxurious picnic, take bottles of water to brew reviving cups of coffee and tea, using an old-fashioned camping kettle heated over an open fire or gas camping stove.*

TOP LEFT *Dome-shaped food nets are efficient at keeping bugs off meat and cheese.*

TOP RIGHT *A basic rectangular plastic lunch box is useful for picnics or carrying sandwiches.*

LEFT *Plain white china is the best neutral backdrop for food.*

putting it all together

Create a lovely colourful, textural outside retreat, where you can unwind on a heap of soft cushions, or soak up the heady scent of a climbing rose. Get in touch with the elements and plant a vegetable patch where you can grow your own nourishing produce. Bring your dining room outside for informal meals, or stretch out on a rug on the grass for a picnic.

Mood

It might sound like a cliché, but it invigorates the senses to be outside, in touch with nature and the elements that surround you: water, light, scent and texture. It is delicious to be in the garden after a terrific rain storm, feeling the cool, damp air and seeing leaves glistening with water, or rose petals plastered to the ground like wet confetti. On long, hot, sunny afternoons, any shady spot becomes a welcome retreat, and it is a luxury to lie in dappled light under a tree, eating an ice-cream or enjoying a lazy picnic. Gardens smell of so many things: fragrant roses and honeysuckle; aromatic herbs like rosemary and lavender, which are very hardy and can be grown just about anywhere; and the heady aroma of damp earth after a storm. Scents are evocative of a time and place, and the fragrance of cut grass or a particular rose can take me back to my childhood. When temperatures soar, the mere sound of water – a tinkling fountain or a gushing outdoor shower or tap – are a relief to a hot and bothered body. Try to find the time to hide away outside in the same way as you might curl up with a good book in a comfortable chair by the fire. Take breakfast outside on a warm and sunny summer's morning, or stretch out on a rug on the grass to catch up with a novel.

LAZY AFTERNOON

Looking back to my childhood, I recall days when we walked to the common and ate ice-creams on a rug under a leafy tree. The parade of shops opposite, their stripy blinds lowered, took on a sleepy feel. Afternoons were long and languid, and best spent in the dappled cool of the large apple tree in our garden reading, drinking lemonade and eating biscuits. Squinting at the afternoon sun from my shady retreat under the awning at our house in Spain, time has passed, but the feeling is the same. With echoes of those carefree days, it is an unsurpassed luxury to soak up the enveloping warmth and enjoy a long, lazy lunch of salads, fresh bread and hunks of cheese, followed by a siesta.

ABOVE AND OPPOSITE
On a long, hot summer's afternoon, keep cool in the dappled light of a shady tree and enjoy a

lazy, informal lunch, with plenty of healthy salads, home-grown vegetables, crispy bread and fresh juicy fruit.

RAIN-SOAKED GARDEN

Sometimes the summer air becomes stuffy and oppressive. The heat intensifies until you feel the first twinges of a headache; you drink litres of water; clothes feel tight and uncomfortable, and it becomes an effort to attempt the simplest chore. Outside, the air draws closer and the light assumes a dull, flat quality. In the garden there is a sense of anticipation; nothing stirs, and the plants seem stifled by the lack of breeze. The air is thick with the dry, scorched smells of grass and earth. The storm clouds gather and darken, and when the first droplets of rain splash and scatter the dusty surface there is a sense of relief. First one drop, then another, and then the sky empties itself like a giant bucket. The thunder rumbles and roars and lightning snakes through the sky. Heavy rain is wonderfully cleansing and leaves the garden sparkling with wetness. It is intoxicating to walk among the dripping plants and drink in the moist, heady, earthy air. Under bare feet the soaking grass feels spongy, cool and more accommodating. Vegetation is greener, and leaves and petals are shiny like pebbles washed by the tide, and the wet paths house small light-reflecting pools. Serious gardeners dread summer storms, which mostly arrive when gardens are at their peak. Yet although it may be disastrous for prize blooms, voluptuous flowers, with drooping petals ready to fall, assume a fragile rain-sodden beauty.

OPPOSITE *Tranquility in a rain-soaked London garden, with rose petals plastered to the ground and the greenery enlivened and intensified in colour.*

ABOVE *Alchemilla bent double with glistening drops of water.*

SCENT

The intoxicating smell of rambling roses, heady jasmine, or the sweetness of cut tuberoses are, like all smells, evocative of a time and place. From my childhood I particularly remember the golden *Rosa* 'Peace' blooms in our garden, which smelt like delicious soap; the fresh, sweet hay-like scent of newly cut grass; and the strange herby smell that lingered on your hands after picking tomatoes. Some of the most aromatic plants are lavender, thyme, camomile and rosemary. Lavender is a hardy evergreen that is easy to grow in pots, or as a decorative hedge or border edging. The spiky stems with their delicate purple summer flowers smell delicious when brushed against. Lavender can be hung in bunches to dry and the flowers used to fill cotton bags to scatter among clothes in drawers. Camomile and thyme are pretty, compact plants that are easy to grow between paving stones and emit fresh, herby fragrances when crushed underfoot. A carpet of camomile on an area of lawn is another delicious way to impart scent. Thyme is good for flavouring meat and fish, while camomile makes a delicious tea. Rosemary is another aromatic plant that is easy to grow and looks pretty either as low hedges, in pots or clipped into topiary standards. I dry stems of rosemary and hang them by the oven to use in cooking. I also use jugs or vases of fresh rosemary stems to decorate summer tables.

ABOVE *Thyme that has been planted in cracks between paving stones adds soft greenery and a delicious, heady scent when it is trodden on and crushed underfoot.*

OPPOSITE *Lavender is aromatic while it is growing, and the dried flowers can be used in lovely scented sachets for drawers and in potpourri mixes.*

ABOVE *Nestling in the shade of an olive tree, a lightweight folding chair, dressed in a simple cotton pull-on loose cover, makes a peaceful retreat – the perfect place to enjoy a quiet hour or two catching up with your novel.*

RIGHT *A shady patch of grass, beneath leafy branches strung with metal candle lanterns, is furnished with a traditional moss-encrusted wooden bench. Next to it, on an old metal table spread with a pink-and-white checked cotton cloth, are bowls of radishes for healthy nibbling.*

SIMPLE RETREATS

Caught up in the demands of work and domestic life in an age that demands our immediate reaction to every bleep of a mobile phone or the arrival of an email, it is important to find time and space to sit, reflect, read a book, or do nothing but soak up the beauty of a warm evening. Make your own peaceful retreat with a favourite chair in the most sensuous part of your garden: by a scented rose, perhaps, or in a spot that gets lots of sun, or in a patch of wild grass and flowers. Set up a table and eat lunch there. My place to hide away from daily demands is my tiny rooftop garden, which is cool and refreshing in the early morning and the perfect place to enjoy breakfast with the radio and newspaper. In the middle of the day I can stretch out on a rug on the decking and soak up some warm sunshine. At dusk I like to watch the sky turn pink, light some candles and relish the peace.

TOP *Folding chairs in pretty colours are practical both inside and outdoors, and are easy to carry to a favourite patch of garden.*

BOTTOM LEFT AND RIGHT *A traditional bench painted a basic garden green colour can be equipped with cushions for extra comfort.*

WATER

It is refreshing to cool off in the heat of the day with an invigorating swim or cold shower. In the scorching midday sun, even the sound of water is a relief to a hot, sticky body. It makes life so much easier if you can install a tap outside for watering plants and to fill bowls of refreshing water to splash you down or soak your feet and hands when the heat becomes too intense. Few of us have the available space or funds required for a swimming pool, but an outside shower is a reasonably inexpensive luxury. Freestanding or fixed to a wall or fence, a simple shower head with a wooden deck beneath is the perfect way to make you feel as if you've just had a reviving dip.

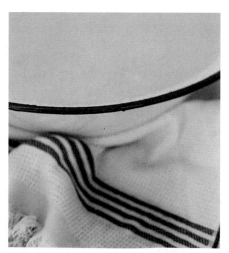

ABOVE AND LEFT *Keep cool with an outside tap, such as this one, which was bought cheaply from a builder's merchant. As well as making watering easy, you can make an impromptu outside washing area with a simple metal bowl, soap and a soft towel.*

OPPOSITE *Install an outside shower to refresh yourself in summer. Mount the shower heads and pipes on a wall or fence tucked away in a secluded corner, and install a suitable surface for drainage, such as a ceramic shower tray or hardwood teak decking.*

SHADY SUMMER'S EVENING

On a balmy evening, move outside to watch the softening light, lengthening shadows and intensifying hues of a technicolour sunset. As dusk falls, it is a peaceful time to sit and reflect on the day's activities. In keeping with this tranquil mood, make your outdoor room a calm oasis furnished in neutral whites and creams. These colours are my favourites for fabrics and furniture on the patio of our house in Spain, where evenings in summer are spent enjoying the fragrant warm air. The table is laid with candles in metal lanterns and vases of tuberoses, and I bring out cream canvas director's chairs, which are really comfortable for lazing in. We light the barbecue, load it with fish steaks and make simple salads of tomatoes and green leaves. In the courtyard, which is lit with more candles in jam jars and lanterns, bench seating is covered with assorted cushions in plain and blue-and-white striped canvas – ideal for stretching out on after a hearty supper.

OPPOSITE *Soft cushions to relax on, in white and understated stripes.*

LEFT *Neutral fabrics brighten the terrace as the light fades at dusk.*

SOFT GRASS

Grass is the perfect outdoor surface for lying on and gazing up at a cloudless summer sky. It comes in many guises: a luxurious stretch of immaculately tended, manicured green lawn, a scorched and bristly playing field, a lush uncultivated field of tall swaying grasses and poppies, or a clipped and cosseted cricket pitch. It is good to feel grass between your toes, or tickling your hands as you idly pick clover and daisies to make into chains. Then there is the wetness of grass early in the morning, glistening with silvery drops of dew, or the soft dampness of a refreshed lawn after a summer rain storm. Pitching camp on a patch of soft, spongy grass is one of the most relaxing ways to spend a hot afternoon at the weekend, and a long, languid picnic will invigorate the soul and improve your mood after the stresses of the week. Some of the best experiences are to be had on a visit to a local park, where you can nearly always find a welcoming shady tree or a secluded sunny patch. Essentials for picnics on the grass are a good cloth to lay your food on and a woolly rug or, if you prefer, some lightweight deck chairs on which to sit.

LEFT *Pack up a picnic tea in a traditional metal lunch box and choose tea-time favourites like flapjacks, bagels and jam, or fruitcake.*

OPPOSITE *Picnic on the grass with a blue-and-white theme: a checked cotton cloth, and deck chairs covered in cheery plain and striped cotton.*

Outside retreats

Many of us, especially urban dwellers, are hemmed in for much of the working day and hardly experience fresh air, let alone the sensations of a crisp and frosty morning or the brilliance of a red sunset. Deprived of natural sensations and smells, we humans get depressed, lethargic and irritable, but our sense of wellbeing increases dramatically when we go outside. Whether it is a terrace, patio, vegetable patch, or even a windowsill with a brimming window box, having an outside space to tend to and enjoy creates a diversion from the irritants of daily life – bills, unwanted phone calls, dirty dishes and so on. Making a room outside – somewhere to eat, drink, sit, contemplate, garden, or play – is no different from decorating and furnishing spaces inside our homes. Outside as well as in, it is important to decide what sort of overall look and feel you wish to create and to be resourceful with your available space. The crucial design aspects still apply, such as what colour to paint walls, what kind of flooring and fabric to choose, and what sort of furniture will work. It is also about creating a little bit of magic to give you a wonderful retreat in which to sit with a book on warm summer evenings or eat croissants and drink steaming coffee in the crisp morning air.

VERANDAS AND PORCHES

I grew up believing that only television characters whiled away warm velvet-dark evenings in rocking chairs on wooden porches, listening to crickets. When I finally visited the USA I saw that it really happens. I am envious that the long, hot summers have made this simple and practical architectural feature a necessity, as well as being a means of enjoying the outside in comfort. Among the neat picket fences and lawns of New England I saw the most charming porches and verandas with pristine white-painted railings and floors. Often enclosed with fine mesh screens to keep out insects, porches are shady retreats where visitors are refreshed with jugs of iced tea and entertained with stories about wild bears. The most stylish and simple porch furniture are old wicker chairs and tables, rocking chairs and hammocks, with faded striped cushions. Some of the best furniture has been bought for just a few dollars from junk shops. In the absence of the real thing, the porch look is easy and inexpensive to achieve using stylish old furniture revamped with paint in funky colours and chair covers and cushions in natural fabrics.

OPPOSITE AND TOP RIGHT *An elegant, shady Long Island porch is painted white and blue and furnished simply with old wicker tables and chairs, with soft feather cushions covered in faded blue-and-white striped ticking.*

LEFT AND RIGHT *Porch style in the barn-red cabins of America's Catskill Mountains makes the most of a selection of simple junk furniture.*

ROOFTOP SPACE

It wasn't until the railings were fixed around the flat roof in the back yard of my London house that I felt it was really and truly an outside room. Before that, there was always a niggling feeling that someone might topple over and, of course, it was out of bounds for children as it was far too dangerous. Apart from installing an outside tap for watering all the container plants, which in summer is essential twice a day, the other important task was to lay the pine decking. With a shady courtyard below, the roof is a welcome suntrap, and for that reason I haven't bothered with awnings – on hot days we make do with wide-brimmed hats and sunglasses to keep the sun off. To make it more sheltered and secretive, clematis, growing in pots, trails around the railings and over a simple trellis painted with pale minty green emulsion. Mixing vegetables with flowers makes gardening a more productive and resourceful occupation, and I like to grow nasturtiums alongside tomatoes and a variety of herbs. Even though the garden is no more than 3.5 square metres, there is a sense of space and freedom high up among the urban rooftops, and there is nothing better than stealing up there to have a bagel and a coffee on a warm summer's morning.

OPPOSITE, BELOW AND RIGHT *Enclosed with green-painted metal railings, this London roof terrace is a welcome suntrap, which is ideal for growing tomatoes, pots of herbs and nasturtiums. The look is simple and utilitarian, with basic tools, old chairs and a table with a green-and-white checked plastic cloth.*

LEFT *A blue-and-white checked rug and some big cushions make a white metal bench a more comfortable proposition.*

BEACH-HUT STYLE

Nearly every seaside town around Britain has a stretch of beach or seafront devoted to higgledy-piggledy strings of small wooden huts that allow you to live, albeit temporarily, in a basic fashion without water or electricity beside the sea. Old-fashioned resorts like Swanage, Bognor, Worthing and Whitstable have great beach huts – the best ones are in isolated spots away from the town centres. Colours vary from place to place: jaunty blue and white; dark brown creosote; ice-cream shades of pistachio, raspberry and mint; and white are all beach-hut paint schemes that will inspire you to create the maritime look at home. Collect pebbles from the beach to make simple seaside still lifes and grow plants like sea kale, which thrive on pebbly beaches, for greenery and texture. My grandmother rented a beach hut in Devon for great informal picnics with scratchy sand on the floor and fishing nets in the corner. Beach-hut kit was appropriately simple: jolly blue-and-white striped canvas deck chairs; a folding table; plain cotton cloths; picnic gear in a wicker basket; a Primus stove to brew hot drinks; and a warm rug for naps.

OPPOSITE, TOP LEFT AND CENTRE *Paint the walls white and rig up a decorative awning in jolly blue-and-white canvas; for practical, stylish seating, use a white slatted folding chair; sea kale growing among pebbles is great for creating texture.*

TOP RIGHT *Traditional beach huts, like these at Worthing, give brilliant ideas for painting a shed or furnishing a deck.*

HOT PATIO

During the long, hot Andalusian summer, all our outside activities take place on the white patio surrounding our house. Rather than opting for rustic limewash, which needs a new coat every spring, we chose basic white matt exterior paint for the walls. The large terracotta tiles underfoot were bought from the local builder's merchant at a very low cost. Furniture is portable so that chairs and tables can be moved according to the time of day. I go to Seville to buy traditional Spanish country chairs and stools with rush seats, which have a timeless appeal. In contrast to the predominately white feel, I like to add splashes of bright colour with shocking-pink napkins or a bright 1940s green-and-turquoise seersucker cloth. Shade is vital, and I designed basic canvas awnings, punched with eyelets and strung to hooks with tough nylon rope.

OPPOSITE *This shady terrace, where the predominance of white is offset by splashes of colourful table linen, is a cool evening retreat.*

THIS PAGE *An awning in blue-and-white striped canvas creates shade on the sun-baked patio.*

URBAN BACK YARD

A plain, simple and utilitarian approach is the key to creating a stylish summer oasis in the confines of a small urban back yard. Rather than being plastered over or repointed, the rough, uneven brick walls have been left to impart their warm, earthy character, together with the worn mossy red-brick pavers that lie underfoot. This natural, neutral backdrop makes cream canvas chair covers an understandable choice, while a simple white cotton cloth dresses up a folding, rather battered, card table. An old wooden meat safe, a mesh food net, a metal flower bucket and tin lanterns hung on the walls are practical and add hard-edged yet decorative detail. An old metal shoe locker makes an impromptu potting shed, with neat shelves for storing

bulbs, pots and tools. A school-room-style jug, plain bowls and robust glasses are ideal for the uncluttered look. Greenery is sparse apart from clematis and some rampant buddleia, so anything other than the small topiary box and an amaryllis in a roughly moulded terracotta pot would be unnecessary.

OPPOSITE AND RIGHT
Utilitarian objects like an old wooden meat safe and a metal shoe locker are useful for storing gardening items in the confines of an urban back yard.

COLOURFUL COURTYARD

A simple way to relieve the drabness of a shady courtyard is to use colourful paint and fabric. I transformed a door with eggshell paint in greenish blue, a colour that is modern, yet fresh and natural. It looked so good that a wall, rebuilt and pointed with ugly cement, was the next contender for the same colour, but in a durable matt emulsion. Ugly water tanks, fences and furniture can also be camouflaged with paint – white is always a good colour to lift a dull, flat environment. Blue-and-white checked cotton is unfailingly cheerful and smart and I used a favourite from my stash of colourful cloths. In a space devoid of many plants, buy colourful flowers like cow parsley, cornflowers or stocks for informal decorations that can be enjoyed outside for several days.

OPPOSITE *Instant greenery is provided by a tall architectural-looking bay standard in a metal bucket.*

LEFT AND ABOVE *Blue-and-white checked table linen, white folding cricket chairs, a vase of pink stocks and a sea-green door add cheerful and contemporary colouring to a shady London courtyard.*

VINE-COVERED TERRACE

A trailing grapevine is a romantic, cool and natural way of shading a terrace. At an ancient Andalusian farmhouse high up among the chestnut and olive groves, four vines, including a knotted and gnarled 20-year-old specimen, have been trained to grow up chestnut posts spaced at 2-metre intervals and across a basic framework of supporting sticks. During the long, hot summers everyone eats under the vines, which sag with bunches of fat, juicy grapes. In early spring when the vines are not in full leaf, the open spaces are filled in with green fabric awning. Locals say that it takes about three years of careful tending and cutting back to make a fully covered vine canopy. Although a vine outside in a colder climate is unlikely to produce such prodigious fruit, it is possible in a sunny, sheltered, south-facing garden to grow impressive leafy examples. For outside living an assortment of seats, like old country chairs and benches, together with new metal garden chairs from department stores, creates a relaxed look. When there are guests to feed, more tables can be brought out under the leafy awning.

FAR LEFT, TOP TO BOTTOM *Ideas for understated, natural-looking window-ledge gardens: a cedar box with aromatic rosemary; painted plastic window boxes planted with ornamental cabbages; lavender in a painted vegetable crate.*

LEFT *Blue-painted pots of geraniums.*

WINDOW-BOX GARDEN

Close to my London home, tubs and pots teeter along the ledges of tower blocks, creating brilliant splashes of colour. These miniature gardens yielding a variety of herbs and vegetables, or gaudy favourites like geraniums and marigolds, are a vibrant sight in an otherwise grim, unrelenting urban environment. Instead of standard containers, be inventive and revamp an old crate with sludgy green paint and plant textural lavender. Green plastic window boxes look functional, but they can also be transformed with matt paint in soft mint green or powder blue. Don't stick to the same old planting material either: a dwarf hedge of rosemary, white hyacinths, nasturtiums or cherry tomatoes are just some ideas that you could adopt for container plantings.

VEGETABLE AND FLOWER PLOT

There is something so satisfying about tending a garden that yields flowers for colour alongside vegetables to eat. This decorative but utilitarian rectangular plot is bordered by a handmade stick fence and yields a combination of floral and edible produce, including clematis, morning glory, sunflowers, lettuces, cabbages, chards and beetroots. In summer, it is a glorious refuge in the cool of early morning or evening, for watering and weeding, soaking up the scents of herbs and enjoying the fresh, bright colours of the young plants.

LEFT *Simple wooden furniture, such as this rustic Adirondack chair, is suitably decorative and functional in a working garden.*

RIGHT *A mixture of colourful flowers and vegetables grow together in this little enclosed garden in America's Catskill Mountains – a truly peaceful oasis in which to sit and contemplate.*

Planting ideas

All gardeners have their own ideas about the key elements in planting a successful space. I view simplicity of layout, together with texture, colour, shape, scent and the edibility of flowers and plants as the most important considerations. I like a sense of order and have a passion for regimented vegetable patches, which have an appeal similar to that of neatly arranged interior rooms. I also like the use of commonplace plants, rather than fancy, exotic varieties that I am happy to leave to real garden experts. Some of my favourites are traditional cottage-garden flowers like roses, dahlias and clematis, as well as all vegetables – especially cabbages, which look so leafy and decorative. The use of containers, from earthy terracotta flowerpots to galvanized metal florist's buckets, is important when space is limited in small yards and on terraces and balconies. Choosing the right size pot, painting it a particular colour, and setting it somewhere appropriate are all important. Planting to create texture and colour with climbing plants or to make a dramatic statement with tall plants, such as sunflowers or topiary trees like box and bay, are also elements that I consider vitally important to creating a living, visually appealing space.

RIGHT AND BELOW *Leeks that have been left to bolt make a dramatic, decorative architectural statement; traditionally used for height in herbaceous borders, delphiniums look good in any setting.*

OPPOSITE, CLOCKWISE FROM TOP LEFT *Sunflowers grow fast and are ideal for creating tall borders; a low white picket fence is bordered by loosestrife for colourful height and detail; hollyhocks look distinctive against plain white walls.*

CREATING HEIGHT

Tall, leggy plants provide drama, height and camouflage. My favourite are sunflowers, which are fun to grow from seed; some varieties reach 3 metres or more, with flowers the size of large plates. Another passion, grown in pots against a wall, are foxgloves, which shoot up with ease to over a metre and have pretty white, purple or pink bell-shaped flowers which bees love. Delphiniums are easy to grow and also have colourful spiky blooms. Other tall plants that are easy to grow include hollyhocks, which have a timeless appeal and look pretty flanking a doorway.

A SENSE OF ORDER

There is something pleasing about small-scale plots with neat rows of vegetables and herbs, tidy flowerbeds with an array of foliage and blooms in colours that blend together or contrast dramatically, and well-raked, weeded soil. It proves that humans can contain nature if they methodically dig, plant and tidy. Create natural order in a decorative yet functional garden, with devices such as pathways – wide enough for a wheelbarrow – made of wood chippings and bordered with lacy flat-leafed parsley, and rows of wonderful old glass bell jars to nurture seedlings. Enclose the area with commonplace yet stylish wire fencing over which climbers like honeysuckle and trailing tomatoes can be entwined.

ABOVE *A makeshift cold frame constructed from salvaged windows is planted with herbs and salad ingredients.*

BELOW AND OPPOSITE *Meticulous well-ordered planting enhances a small ornamental and practical vegetable and flower garden.*

POTTING IDEAS

A terracotta pot is hard to beat as a container for everything from bulbs to shrubs and herbs. The earthiest pots are the old, roughly moulded, hand-thrown ones that are more textural than machine-produced models. Interesting containers are not difficult to find. Raid your local hardware shop for galvanized metal buckets, which look great with topiary standards of box, bay or rosemary, but drill holes for drainage. Bear in mind that the simplest arrangements of only two or three pots can be the most effective. Galvanized troughs look modern and functional on windowsills planted with pretty flowers like hyacinths, narcissi, ornamental cabbages or herbs.

OPPOSITE *Metal buckets from a hardware shop look particularly effective in small groups.*

ABOVE *Almost anything with an earthy, organic look will do as a container for plants, from traditional terracotta flowerpots or an old sink to galvanized metal troughs.*

CLIMBERS

Train climbing plants with wire and garden string along walls, fences and trellises, and up pergolas, arbours and wigwam-shaped structures. As well as creating colour and greenery in a skyward direction, climbers are useful for camouflaging unattractive surfaces. I grow clematis in pots, which runs rampant over the rails around my roof garden and trails up a trellis over a section of harsh red brick wall. The plants soften the hard urban landscape, existing very well in terracotta pots if fed regularly with manure and watered copiously. Other favourite climbers include plumbago, which has beautiful star-like flowers; climbing roses like *Rosa* 'Madame Alfred Carrière' and *R.* 'New Dawn'; grapevines, which are perfect for making shady arbours; jasmine, especially varieties that produce the most wonderful heady scent at night; and passion flowers — I love the purplish blooms and orange fruits. Climbers are also handy if space is short. In a vegetable plot, for example, nasturtiums, tomatoes, beans, cucumbers and courgettes can all be trained up stakes and along fences.

OPPOSITE, CLOCKWISE FROM FAR LEFT *A moss rose trained with string and wire; climbing runner beans; stick fencing supports tomatoes; nasturtiums growing up pea sticks; clematis and other climbers trail over chicken wire, creating a leafy paradise for hens.*

LEFT *Pretty plumbago climbing up fine wires.*

Floppy green cabbages planted with a colourful array of dahlias in a working garden in London are good examples of combined floral and edible produce.

LEFT AND OPPOSITE *This ornamental flower and vegetable patch in the Catskill Mountains in America measures just 6.5 x 9 metres. It is bisected with hard-earth paths and planted with neat rows of lettuces, chard and cabbages, interspersed with colourful blooms such as daisies and vibrant marigolds.*

FLOWERS AND VEGETABLES

For economic reasons, traditional cottage gardens always contained a mixture of flowers for cutting and vegetables for consumption by the family. Many gardeners, who are not necessarily interested in self-sufficiency, adopt the same approach for purely decorative reasons, since many vegetables and herbs hold ornamental appeal. Others, who enjoy eating the fruits of their labours, delight in growing a combination of the decorative and the edible, with everything from beans and potatoes to roses and sweet peas jostling for position in one patch. I look forward to late summer, when tiny plots are ablaze with colour in the form of big, floppy green cabbages and lettuces, contrasted with the gaudy pinks, yellows and oranges of dahlias. For dramatic contrast, plant round-headed lettuces next to tall, gangly alliums with their pompom flowers. A combination of chives, mint and parsley can be used to create pretty, textural edgings, while tall climbing plants like beans, tomatoes and cucumbers make attractive green perimeters. Layers of straw mulch also looks decorative.

LEFT AND BELOW *An apple tree from an espaliered row enclosing a simple vegetable and herb garden. A wigwam-shaped wire topiary frame for climbing plants like ivy, nasturtiums, vine tomatoes or beans; as the plant grows, the stems can be trained around the wire and tied in place with string.*

OPPOSITE, LEFT TO RIGHT *An aromatic rosemary standard is trimmed into an architectural shape – the clippings can be dried for use in cooking; a squat box ball looks good on its own or arranged with others on a balcony or terrace.*

CLIPPED AND TRAINED

When we think of topiary it is usually yew hedges clipped into amusing animal shapes. On a smaller scale – available from any good garden centre – there are evergreen shrubs like box and bay clipped into squat balls or taller, leggy stems with pom-pom tops. These all look good in small paved areas and require very little maintenance apart from watering and regular trimming with shears to keep them in shape. There are topiary wire frames in wigwam and ball shapes that are good for training things like vine tomatoes, beans and nasturtiums. In the walled gardens of old country houses, you often see the espaliered branches of exotic pear and apple varieties that have been trained to grow flat and spread out in fan shapes. An espalier framework is made with a series of upright posts supporting several wires strained horizontally to secure the branches. An espalier-trained tree is restricted to pairs of branches that stretch out horizontally from the trunk and are secured to the espalier for support. Espaliered trees also make an unusual natural fence or partition in a small garden.

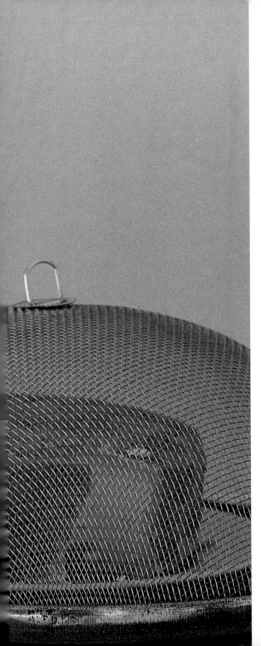

Eating outside

Eating and drinking are sensual pleasures, and become more so if the ingredients are delicious and the surroundings heavenly. Simplicity is the key to making the most of a balmy evening or a sunny afternoon. Invest in good, basic cooking tools, such as sharp knives, solid mixing bowls and pans with heavy bases. Keep tableware simple with plain white china and durable but good-looking glassware – something like Duralex is perfect. Use white sheets for everyday tablecloths, but for special occasions splash out on beautiful crisp linen. Buy the best cheese, fish, meat, fruit, vegetables and wine that you can afford, and prepare meals that involve minimal preparation. Serve lots of healthy salads and raw vegetables and enjoy experimenting with the addition of home-grown herbs. Set the table in a sheltered, shady environment and keep furniture basic and portable: a trestle table and folding director's chairs are ideal. At night, light candles in lanterns, jam jars or glass holders, and decorate the table with jugs of freshly cut herbs or flowers such as roses or marigolds. Keep picnic equipment to a minimum, with a cool box, rug and corkscrew. Set up camp under a tree or in a sheltered sand dune and build a fire to cook sausages or pack plenty of bagels and good chocolate and wine.

PICNICS

My family are enthusiastic picnickers who relish the freedom of eating informally outside at any time of year. We head off to one of the parks in London, or, when we need to blow away the cobwebs, we go further afield to a safe, sandy beach, such as Camber Sands in Sussex or Studland Bay in Dorset. The best picnics are simple and uncomplicated affairs.

For meals by the sea, I pack a basket with napkins, a box of matches and a bottle cooler. In a sheltered spot by a breakwater or in a sand dune, we make a campfire with driftwood and dried seaweed or light a little metal barbecue for a cook-up after a dip in the sea. Fried eggs or sausages are wedged between chunks of good chewy bread. Sometimes we buy a local dressed crab, which, seasoned with lemon and pepper, we spread onto wholewheat bread. On cold but bright winter days, I pack a warm wool tartan blanket, bars of good chocolate, a flask of potato and leek soup, and a box of bagels with smoked salmon and cream cheese. Other picnic goodies include wedges of delicious cheese with oatcakes and cheese straws, chunks of tomatoes dipped in a little salt, a jar of olives, large chunks of cucumber and crisp apples.

OPPOSITE, CLOCKWISE FROM
TOP LEFT *A perfect picnic,
quick and easy to prepare:
cucumber chunks; bread
with fresh crab; and eggs
frying on a campfire.*

THIS PAGE *A picnic by the
sea on the deck of a beach
hut is simple and stylish
with a white folding chair,
blue-and-white napkins,
and a big straw basket.*

RIGHT AND OPPOSITE *Simple food suits the pared-down look of an outdoor table, with white cloth, basic tableware, mesh food nets, candles in glass holders and a few stems of tuberose.*

BELOW, TOP TO BOTTOM *Roasted peppers and aubergines; roast diced potatoes; tomatoes with olive oil and basil.*

SIMPLE SUPPER

rocket or other seasonal leaves are essential, as are home-grown tomatoes, chopped up with basil, garlic, salt, lemon juice and olive oil. In keeping with my pared-down approach to cooking, I cover the table with a crisp white cloth and serve food in large white enamelled metal dishes, which look stylish alongside simple plain white crockery.

I have a passion for vegetables, especially roasted, and find them one of the simplest, tastiest accompaniments to grilled or barbecued fish and meat. For summer suppers, I chop up potatoes, complete with skins, aubergines, red peppers, onions and courgettes, and place them in a flat roasting pan with a good douse of olive oil and lemon juice, some garlic, rosemary or basil, and cook them in the middle of a hot oven, turning regularly, for about 45 minutes or until everything is soft and nicely browned. Any leafy green vegetable, such as cabbage, is delicious steamed, then cooked for a minute or so in butter and mint. Staples like baked potatoes, impaled on a skewer for faster cooking, are another favourite served with butter, salt and pepper. Salads of lettuce,

LUNCH BREAK

When I am dashing about for work, grabbing sandwiches to eat on the run, I think wistfully of my Spanish friends who sit down daily to a relaxing and civilized lunch, either at home where they tuck into something like a tortilla, or in a bar that serves delicious tapas of squid or fried fish. Things are happily different on holiday, when there is time to sit down to eat and talk in the middle of the day. Pasta is the top request in my household and, as long as there is a good bed of steaming al dente spaghetti to mix the sauce in, I can get away with ingredients that are otherwise unacceptable to the youngest members, such as strong cheese, herbs and, worst of all, lots of garlic. Tomato sauce, made with tasty home-grown or field tomatoes, is one of the easiest and most delicious things to serve with pasta. Simply fry three or four large, peeled, chopped tomatoes in olive oil and garlic until they are half cooked. Seasoned with parsley or basil, this highly aromatic, slightly crunchy, tomato sauce is best with a long pasta like tagliatelle or spaghetti. As soon as pumpkins are available in late summer, I cook a kilo or so of the chopped flesh in salted water until soft. After draining, I fry it in olive oil and garlic for a few minutes, and then add half a small pot of single cream, 30 grams of grated Parmesan, and some nutmeg or basil to bring out the flavour of the pumpkin. Then I pulverize the mixture in a blender. When heated up, this utterly delicious pale-orange sauce can be served with any pasta. Fresh wild mushrooms cooked in butter, garlic and parsley are another delicious accompaniment for pasta. Vegetable lasagne is also a favourite.

THIS PAGE AND OPPOSITE
Make simple lunch-time pasta treats with chopped home-grown tomatoes and herbs, served with a wedge of fresh bread and a glass of cold white wine.

BIRTHDAY PARTY

It is wishful thinking to imagine that junk food like crisps, sweets and fizzy drinks are not expected at a children's party. When my daughter requested pizza for her sixth birthday party, I felt mean when I refused her the bought kind that ooze preservatives, which she had set her sights on. So I was faced with the challenge of producing healthy pizza that would please a disgruntled birthday girl. I cut thick slices of crusty bread and toasted them on one side. Then I rubbed the uncooked side with garlic, trickled on olive oil, and added cooked chopped tomatoes. I topped the slices with grated Parmesan and placed them under the grill until bubbling – a great success. I gave in and bought bottles of the least violently coloured lemonade, but offered jugs of iced water, too, which were just as popular. I also served slices of watermelon and orange, cold from the fridge. We made an outrageously rich chocolate biscuit cake, which was decorated with blackberries and candles. Rather than using plain paper plates and cups, I bought brightly coloured plastic plates, cups and straws from a local discount shop, and laid the table with a length of bright-blue plastic cloth.

THIS PAGE AND OPPOSITE *Chocolate biscuit cake and home-made pizza are key ingredients for a children's birthday party. Plastic, in bright colours for the tablecloth, plates, beakers and straws, is both practical and festive tableware and creates a fun and welcoming setting.*

TEA TIME

A glorious summer's afternoon is a wonderful excuse to make something sticky and sweet to eat outside with a cup of steaming and refreshing Earl Grey tea. Make this indulgent treat a vibrant occasion with a jazzy orange tablecloth and a jug of bright marigolds, zinnias or roses. For a traditional English tea, make bite-size cucumber and cream cheese sandwiches. Bake some fairy cakes – they really are very simple and quick to make. Mix together 125 grams caster sugar, 2 eggs and 175 grams self-raising flour, then spoon heaped teaspoons of the mixture into little paper cases or greased bun tins and bake at 180°C (350°F), gas mark 4, for ten minutes. When the cakes are cool, decorate them with icing and fresh or crystallized flower petals, like pansy, rose, marigold, nasturtium, geranium, lavender and borage. Other tea-time goodies include freshly baked scones, which can be thrown together in a matter of minutes. Simply mix 250 grams self-raising flour, 50 grams butter, 50 grams caster sugar, l beaten egg and 75 ml milk in a bowl. Roll out the dough, cut it into rounds, then place them on a greased baking tray and cook at 230°C (450°F), gas mark 8, for ten minutes. Try serving them warm with crème fraîche and home-made blackberry jam. Flapjacks, made with golden syrup, butter and rolled oats, are deliciously chewy, and another favourite is crumbly shortbread.

ABOVE *Delicious fairy cakes are decorated with icing and fresh marigold petals.*

OPPOSITE *A vibrant tea-time table setting with contemporary colour provided by the pink and orange tablecloth, napkins and wool throw. A vase of marigolds and roses adds an extra brilliant touch of colour.*

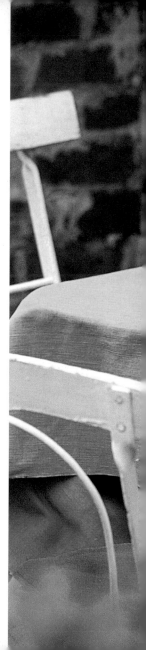

RIGHT AND OPPOSITE *Pale blue-and-white stripes combined with minty green is a stylish and understated colour scheme that is perfect for eating out on a wooden veranda. The folding director's chairs are covered in tough canvas and can be stored away easily at the end of summer. Simple metal hurricane lanterns, and jugs of blue scabious and cornflowers complete the simple, relaxed effect.*

SUMMER PUDDINGS

With so many fruits in season – strawberries, cherries and gooseberries – making delicious puddings for summer meals has endless possibilities and can be really simple. My favourite fruit fool, made with thick cream or low-fat fromage frais, is good old-fashioned gooseberry, which I serve with shortbread; other successful fools include lemon, quince and blackberry. Tarts are always a good idea, and, made with plums, peaches or apples in a rich, buttery pastry case like pâte sucrée, they are delicious hot or cold. Real fruit jellies made with gelatine and fresh raspberry, strawberry, peach or grape juice, look really pretty in individual glasses. There is also a traditional basin-shaped summer pudding, perfect for when all the berry fruits are in season, such as red and black currants, raspberries and blueberries.

BREAKFAST

Good coffee, fresh bread, butter and home-made jam are my essentials for a civilized breakfast. I like to make strong Italian espresso coffee in an old-fashioned percolator, and, unless the bread is still warm from the bakery, I prefer it heated up in the oven or toasted. There are so many fancy breads to choose from nowadays, but toasted hunks from a healthy wholemeal loaf or a crusty white loaf are as tasty as they are filling, and I think just as good as the fancier varieties. Breakfast time is a chance to indulge in eating natural honey and home-made jams and marmalades. When bitter Seville oranges are in season in January, I always promise myself I will make a batch of marmalade, which, interestingly, the Spanish themselves don't eat and consider it a curious British habit that they don't understand. Fresh fruit on the table – figs, watermelon, peaches and apples in the summer, and fat, juicy oranges in the winter – is always a treat for me, and an easy alternative source of vitamin C is a large glass of unsweetened orange juice. Unless it is the weekend or a holiday, I like breakfast to be a fairly quick and efficient meal, with basic white plates and mugs set on a practical, yet jolly, plastic checked cloth.

ABOVE AND OPPOSITE *An alfresco breakfast of fresh fruit, bread and honey, washed down with a cup of strong black coffee, is a perfect way to start the day.*

Simple white plates and mugs set on a practical plastic cloth are also key elements, while shade is provided by basic home-made cream canvas awnings.

CREDITS

Page 7 Ash pergola in the garden of Dean Riddle, Phoenicia, NY, USA.
Page 12 Paint swatches from top: Marston & Langinger Warm White; Sanderson Spectrum 4–19 Winter White; Sanderson Spectrum 3–19 Sunny White; Marston & Langinger Ivory; Jelly glass, After Noah.
Page 113 Wooden picket-fence window box, Jerry's Home Store.
Page 14 Blue-and-white checked place mat, Crate & Barrel, USA.
Page 15 Paint swatches from top: Marston & Langinger Silver Blue; Sanderson Spectrum 24–15 Blue Day; Sanderson Spectrum 25–22 Columbine; Sanderson Spectrum 54–23 King's Blue.
Page 16 Paint swatches from top: Marston & Langinger Pistachio; Sanderson Spectrum 40–04 Sunny Green; Sanderson Spectrum 34–20 Grey Green Light; Farrow & Ball no. 32 Cooking Apple Green.
Page 18 Wool rug, Designers Guild; cricket chair, IKEA; tulips, McQueens; paint swatches from top: Brats no. 105 Constantinople; Sanderson Spectrum 21–10 Fidelity; Sanderson Spectrum 21–04 Lilac; Sanderson Spectrum 23–05 Easter Egg.
Page 21 Paint swatches from top: Marston & Langinger Verona Pink; Brats no. 100 Cairo; Brats no. 108 Seville; Marston & Langinger Terracotta; flowerpots, Smith & Hawken, USA.
Page 21 Scented candles, Price's Patent Candle Co; napkins, Designers Guild; plastic plate and cutlery, Woolworth's.
Page 22 Yellow bowl, El Corte Ingles, Spain.
Page 23 Paint swatches from top: Marston & Langinger Sand; Marston & Langinger Bamboo; Farrow & Ball no. 51 Sudbury Yellow; Sanderson Spectrum 6–23 Gobi Tan; napkin and place mat, Crate & Barrel, USA.
Pages 24–5 House of Ellen O'Neill, Long Island, NY, USA.
Page 32 Garden of Timothy Leese and Robert Chance, Norfolk; blue and green PVC, Habitat; deck chair in checked cotton fabric by Designers Guild; gate in the garden of Nancy McCabe, northwest Connecticut, USA.
Page 33 Stick border (bottom left) and stick fencing (bottom right) in the garden of Dean Riddle, Phoenicia, NY, USA.
Page 34 Shed in the allotment garden of John Matheson, London.
Page 36–7 Fence painted in Prion outdoor paint by Crown-Berger in the garden of Vanessa de Lisle, Fashion Consultant, London.
Page 37 stick fencing (bottom right) in the garden of Dean Riddle, Phoenicia, NY, USA.
Page 38–9 Metal plant trough, The Conran Shop.
Page 40–1 Weathered terracotta flowerpots, General Trading Company.
Page 41 centre low planter & rhubarb forcer, Avant Garden; below left hanging pot, Clifton Nurseries, with a wash of white and terracotta emulsion by Cole & Son; below centre old flowerpot with amaryllis, The Conran Shop; below right long tom, Avant Garden.
Page 42 top left metal planter, The Conran Shop; centre metal lunch box, Muji; below left metal bucket with lavender, Paula Pryke Flowers; below right metal bucket, G J Chapman.
Page 43 left metal bucket, IKEA.
Page 44 Green and blue plastic flowerpots, The Conran Shop.
Page 45 Wooden picket-fence window box, Jerry's Home Store; plastic window box, Clifton Nurseries, painted in powder blue emulsion by Farrow & Ball; ornamental cabbages, McQueens.
Page 60–1 Bench painted in colour 819 by Benjamin Moore & Co, USA.
Page 62–3 1 ribbed cotton, The Conran Shop; 2 cotton, Sanderson; 3 linen, Sanderson; PVC-coated cotton, John Lewis; 5 checked sheer cotton, Habitat; 6 washed cotton, The Conran Shop; 7 plain dye canvas cotton, John Lewis; 8 cotton duck, Whaleys Ltd; 9 cotton, Habitat; 10 cotton, Designers Guild; 11 ribbed cotton, The Conran Shop; 12 silk, Designers Guild; 13 ribbed cotton, stylist's own; 14 ribbed cotton, The Conran Shop; 15 cotton ticking, Ian Mankin; 16 cotton, Ian Mankin; 17 striped cotton, Laura Ashley; 18 checked cotton, Ian Mankin; 19 cotton ticking, Ian Mankin; 20 PVC-coated viscose and polyester, John Lewis; 21 solid rib caustic cotton, Habitat; 22 plain cotton, Designers Guild; 23 cotton check, Designers Guild; 24 sheer cotton, Habitat; 25 PVC, Habitat; 26 PVC Habitat; 27 PVC, Habitat.
Page 64 From top blue wooden bench, IKEA; aluminium-frame rocking chair, Graham & Green; old deck chair in green cotton check, Designers Guild.
Page 65 From top left potting bench, IKEA, painted in Monsoon 1030, Dulux Definitions; deck chair, Jerry's Home Store; sun-lounger with aluminium frame, Graham & Green: folding table, IKEA.
Pages 66–7 Jug, Ruby Beets Antiques, USA.
Page 68 Top lantern, B'zar; below left hurricane lantern, Jerry's Home Store; below right nightlight, IKEA.
Page 69 Left candles, Price's Patent Candle Co; centre right glass storm lamp, The Dining Room Shop; below right glass storm lamps, Jerry's Home Store.

Page 70 From top shears, Avant Garden; besom broom, Avant Garden; trug, Clifton Nurseries; dibber and fork, Clifton Nurseries.

Page 71 From top plastic apron and gardening gloves, Homebase; holdall, Wellington boots with leather lining, Avant Garden; Homebase; plastic refuse bag, Homebase; wooden plant labels, The Conran Shop; raffia and string, Homebase; Andalusian pitchfork and old spade, Avant Garden.

Page 72 From top white plastic bowl, Divertimenti; bottle cooler, Blacks Camping Shop; wooden tray, Habitat, painted in Sanderson Spectrum 23–05 Easter Egg; plastic mug, Debenhams; Duralex glass, The Conran Shop; metal jug, Jerry's Home Store; water jug, Staines Catering Equipment.

Page 73 From top tin plate, Blacks Camping Shop; Greek barbecue, Young & D; plastic plate, knife and fork, Woolworth's; gingham paper napkins, Paperchase; orange-and-pink checked napkin, Designers Guild; food net, Divertimenti; plastic lunch box, Divertimenti; white bowl, Staines Catering Equipment; kettle, stylist's own.

Page 76–7 Garden of Vanessa de Lisle, Fashion Consultant, London.

Page 78–9 Garden of Lisa Bynon and Mona Nehrenberg, Sag Harbor, NY, USA.

Pages 80–1 Garden of Vanessa de Lisle, Fashion Consultant, London.

Page 84 Cloth in checked cotton by Designers Guild.

Page 86 Bowl and cotton towel, The Conran Shop.

Page 87 garden of Lisa Bynon and Mona Nehrenberg, Sag Harbor, NY, USA.

Page 88 White folding table painted in white emulsion, Habitat; cushions in bold striped cotton by Laura Ashley and narrow striped cotton by Ian Mankin.

Page 89 Folding director's chairs, Heal's.

Page 90 Metal lunch box, Muji.

Page 91 Checked cloth, Divertimenti.

Page 92–3 Chairs and cotton covers, The Conran Shop.

Page 94 House of Ellen O'Neill, Long Island, NY, USA.

Page 95 Blue-and-white striped cotton cushion covers, Ralph Lauren Home Collection, USA; top house of Ellen O'Neill, Long Island, NY, USA; bottom left and right: house of Dean Riddle, Phoenicia, NY, USA.

Page 97 top left blue checked wool blanket, Melin Tregwynt; below metal sieve, After Noah; chair and wooden trellis painted in Sanderson Spectrum 39–03 Salad Green; checked plastic fabric tablecloth, John Lewis; watering can, Tobias and the Angel.

Page 100 Blue-and-green cloth, Tobias and the Angel; jug, The Conran Shop; folding cricket chairs, Habitat.

Page 101 Wooden folding table, Habitat.

Page 102 Folding chairs, Habitat, with covers made in cotton duck from Whaleys Ltd; food net, Divertimenti; wooden food safe, After Noah.

Page 103 Metal shoe locker, After Noah.

Page 104 Metal bucket, IKEA; bay tree, Clifton Nurseries.

Page 105 Cloth in blue checked cotton, Designers Guild; white bowl, The Conran Shop.

Page 106–7 Garden of Nick and Hermione Tudor, Finca El Moro, Spain.

Page 108 Top left cedar window box, Clifton Nurseries; location: house of David and Carolyn Fuest, London; centre left plastic window boxes, Clifton Nurseries, painted in powder blue emulsion by Farrow & Ball.

Page 109 Vegetable and flower plot of Dean Riddle, Phoenicia, NY, USA.

Page 112 Blue bench, IKEA.

Page 113 top left allotment garden of John Matheson, London.

Page 115 Vegetable and flower garden of Nancy McCabe, northwest Connecticut, USA.

Page 116 Metal buckets, IKEA and G J Chapman; small metal bin, Paula Pryke Flowers.

Page 117 Metal planters, The Conran Shop.

Page 118 Chicken coop in the garden of Nancy McCabe, northwest Connecticut, USA; stick fencing in the garden of Dean Riddle, Phoenicia, NY, USA.

Page 121 Vegetable and flower garden of Dean Riddle, Phoenicia, NY, USA.

Page 122 Herb and vegetable garden of Nancy McCabe, northwest Connecticut, USA.

Page124–5 Glasses, El Corte Ingles, Spain; food net, Divertimenti.

Page128–9 Food nets, Ruby Beet Antiques, USA; storm lamps, Habitat; jug and bowl, The Conran Shop; metal flower bucket, The Conran Shop.

Page I31 Folding cricket chairs and wooden folding tables painted in white emulsion, Habitat.

Page 132–3 Tablecloth in blue PVC fabric from Habitat; straws, IKEA.

Page 134–5 Checked rug and checked napkins, Designers Guild; cloth in orange cotton fabric from The Conran Shop.

Page 136 Metal hurricane lanterns, Jerry's Home Store; metal jug, Jerry's Home Store; striped cloth and napkins, Jerry's Home Store; folding chairs, Old Town;jelly glasses, After Noah.

Page 137 Tray, Habitat, painted in Sanderson Spectrum 23–05 Easter Egg.

Page 138 White plates, IKEA.

SUPPLIERS

CONTAINERS

The Chelsea Gardener, 125 Sydney Street, London SW3 6NR, 020 7352 5656, www.chelseagardener.com
Terracotta, plastic and wood, pots, urns and window boxes.
Clifton Nurseries, 5a Clifton Villas, London W9 2PH, 020 7289 6851, www.clifton.co.uk
Terracotta and window boxes.

FABRIC FOR AWNINGS, COVERS AND CUSHIONS

Anta, www.anta.co.uk
Hard-wearing picnic rugs and blankets.
Laura Ashley, www.lauraashley.com
Coloured cottons in stripes or checks.
Designers Guild, 267–271 & 277 King's Road, London SW3 5EN, 020 7351 5775, www.designersguild.com
Bright cottons in florals and checks.
Cath Kidston, www.cathkidston.com
1950s-inspired cotton vinyl.
MacCulloch & Wallis, 25–26 Dering Street, London W1R 0BH, www.macculloch.com
Silks for cushions and loose covers.
Malabar Cotton Co Ltd, 31–33 The South Bank Business Centre, Ponton Road, London SW8 5BL, 020 7501 4200, www.malabar.co.uk
Checked, striped and plain cottons.
Ian Mankin, 109 Regents Park Road, London NW1 8UR, 020 7722 0997
Cotton checks and stripes. Mail order catalogue.
Melin Tregwynt, www.melintregwynt.co.uk
Wool throws and blankets.

FENCING, TRELLIS AND GATES

Buckingham Nursery, 57 Tingewick Road, Buckingham MK18 4AE, www.hedging.co.uk
Beech, hazel and holly hedging.
Clifton Nurseries, 5a Clifton Villas, London W9 2PH, www.clifton.co.uk
Simple wooden trellis.

English Hurdle, www.hurdle.co.uk
Willow hurdle fencing.

FURNITURE AND ACCESSORIES

Blacks, www.blacks.co.uk
Tin mugs and Swiss army knives.
Chalwyn Ltd, www.chalwyn.co.uk
Traditional metal hurricane lamps.
The Conran Shop, Michelin House, 81 Fulham Road, London SW3 6RD, www.conran.co.uk
Lanterns, galvanized metal buckets, terracotta pots, plant labels, tools, folding chairs, tables and hammocks.
Designers Guild, 267–271 & 277 King's Road, London SW3 5EN, 020 7351 5775, www.designersguild.com
Coloured table linen plus cushions, tableware and baskets.
Habitat, www.habitat.net
Seasonal garden furniture.
John Lewis, www.johnlewis.com
Garden furniture in season.
Muji, www.muji.co.uk
Folding canvas and metal chairs, plus plates, cups and metal lunch boxes.
Price's Patent Candle Co Ltd, 110 York Road, London SW11 3RU, 020 7924 6336, www.prices-candles.co.uk
Huge selection of candles.

HARD SURFACES

Dorset Reclamation, www.dorsetrec.u-net.com
Reclaimed flagstones, paving bricks, and quarry tiles.
Fired Earth, www.firedearth.co.uk
Spanish terracotta tiles.
Adrian Hall, The Garden Centre, Feltham Hill Road, Feltham, Middlesex TW13 7NA, 020 8890 1778
Old red-brick Tudor tiles and Victorian paving setts.
Habibi, 1c, Greyhound Rd (off Harrow Road), London NW10 5QH, 020 8960 9203, www.habibi.co.uk
Glazed Moroccan terracotta tiles for the garden.
Leisuredeck Ltd, www.leisuredeck.co.uk
Western red cedar timber decking.

Ribble Reclamation, www.ribble-reclamation.co.uk
York flagstones, cobbles and other reclaimed architectural items.
Solopark, www.solopark.co.uk
Reclaimed building materials, plus old red-brick pavers for paths and courtyards.

OUTSIDE EATING

Debenhams, www.debenhams.co.uk
The Dining Room Shop, 62–64 White Hart Lane, 020 8878 1020
Divertimenti, www.divertimenti.co.uk
Graham & Green, 4 & 10 Elgin Crescent, London W11 2JA, 020 7727 4594, www.grahamandgreen.co.uk
Habitat, www.habitat.net
IKEA, www.ikea.co.uk
David Mellor, 4 Sloane Square, London SW1W 8EE, 020 7730 4259, www.davidmellordesign.co.uk
The Pier, www.pier.co.uk
Summerill and Bishop, 100 Portland Road, London W11 4LN, 020 7221 4566
Woolworth's, www.woolworths.co.uk

PAINTS

Cole & Son Ltd, www.cole-and-son.co.uk
Period paint colours for walls and pots.
Crown, www.crownpaint.co.uk
Wide range of colours and finishes.
Dulux, www.dulux.co.uk
Huge range of colours and textures.
Farrow & Ball Ltd, www.farrow-ball.co.uk
National Trust colours; Cooking Apple Green is particularlygood on garden trellis and furniture.
Marston & Langinger, 192 Ebury Street, London SW1W 8UP, 020 7881 5783, www.marston-and-langinger.com
Good colours in finishes designed for outside use.
John Oliver, 33 Pembridge Road, London W11 3HG, 020 7221 6466, www.johnoliver.co.uk
Excellent colours for garden furniture.

Sanderson,
www.sanderson-online.co.uk
Wide range of paint colours.

PLANTS AND SEEDS
David Austin Roses,
www.davidaustinroses.com
Climbing roses and modern bush roses.
Blooms of Bressingham,
Bressingham, Diss, Norfolk, IP22 2AB,
01379 688 585,
www.bloomsofbressingham.co.uk
Plants and bulbs.
Clifton Nurseries, 5a Clifton Villas,
London W9 2PH, 020 7289 6851,
www.clifton.co.uk
Everything for a well-furnished garden.
Columbia Road Flower Market,
Columbia Road, London E2 (Bethnal
Green or Old Street tube)
Market held every Sunday morning –
cheap bulbs, cut flowers and plants.
Croftway Nursery,
www.croftway.co.uk
Bearded irises, hardy geraniums and
other perennials.
Deacons Nursery, Moor View,
Godshill, Ventnor, Isle of Wight,
PO38 3HW, 01983 840750
Fruit trees.
Future Foods, www.futurefoods.co.uk
Unusual vegetables and edible plants
from seed and tubers.
Grooms, www.grooms-flowers.co.uk
Bulbs for autumn and spring planting.
Halls Nursery,
www.hallsofheddon.co.uk
Dahlia specialist.
Hexham Herbs,
www.chesterswalledgarden.co.uk
Herb specialist.
Langley Boxwood Nursery,
www.boxwood.co.uk
Box hedges and topiary for pots.
Parkers Dutch Bulbs,
www.jparkers.co.uk
Specialize in tulips.
Reads Nursery,
www.readsnursery.co.uk
Fig plants, asparagus, sweet oranges,
lavender, wisteria and plumbago.

Cottage Garden Roses,
www.cottagegardenroses.com
Old-fashioned roses.
Sandeman Seeds,
www.sandemanseeds.com
Seeds of rare plants.
Scotts Nurseries, Merriott, Somerset
TA16 5PL, 01460 72306
Apple trees; figs, nuts, walnuts and
rhubarb, plus climbing roses, old-
fashioned roses, violas, delphiniums,
peonies, and clematis.
Simpson's Seeds,
www.simpsonsseeds.co.uk
Basil, broad beans, tomatoes. Plastic
solar domes to protect seedlings.
Thompson & Morgan,
www.thompson-morgan.com
Seed specialists, including vegetables
and blooms such as sunflowers.

SHEDS AND GREENHOUSES
Garden Chic, www.gardenchic.co.uk
Classic summerhouses and log cabins.
Greenhouses Direct,
www.greenhousesdirect.co.uk
Huge range of greenhouses.
Homebase, www.homebase.co.uk
Simple garden sheds.
Langhale Gardens,
www.langhalegardens.co.uk
Sheds, greenhouses and playhouses.

SOIL AND MANURE
Banks Horticultural Products, Angel
Court, Dairy Yard, High Street, Market
Harborough, Leicestershire LE16 7NL,
01858 464346
Deliver top soil in the Midlands only.
Fairfield Turf, Fairfield Court,
Brookland, Romney Marsh,
Kent TN29 9RX, 01797 344731
Soils and turf delivered nationally.
The Organic Gardening Catalogue,
www.organiccatalog.com
Organic green manure and compost,
seaweed meal and organic fertilizer.
Also organic seeds and plants.

TOOLS AND OTHER ACCESSORIES
Alitag Plant Labels, 131 Bourne Lane,
Much Hadham, Hertfordshire SG10
6ER, 01279 842685
Aluminium labels for plant names.
The Essentials Company,
www.essentialscompany.co.uk
Aluminium, slate and wooden labels.
The Garden Trading Company,
www.gardentrading.co.uk
A wide range of gardening tools.
The General Trading Company, 144
Sloane Street, London SW1X 9BL, 020
7730 0411, www.general-trading.co.uk
Garden accessories.
Gone Gardening,
www.gonegardening.com
Haemmerlin galvanized wheelbarrows,
garden ornaments and tools.
Haws Watering Cans,
www.haws.co.uk
Old-fashioned metal watering cans.
The Heveningham Collection,
www.heveningham.co.uk
Hand-crafted iron furniture.
Hortus Ornamenti,
www.hortus-ornamenti.co.uk
Hand-made traditional garden tools.
Labour and Wait,
www.labourandwait.co.uk
Forged steel secateurs, Haws metal
watering cans and enamel exterior
thermometers.
Manufactum,
www.manufactum.co.uk
Bell jars, plant protectors, zinc plant
labels and seedling trays.
Windrush Mill Catalogue, House 2
Rivers Est, Witney, Oxford, Oxon, OX8
6BA, 01993 770500
Wheelbarrows and terracotta long tom
pots.

INDEX

ACKNOWLEDGMENTS

It has been enormous fun putting together *Pure Style Outside*. It would not have been possible without all the hard work and support from everyone at Ryland Peters and Small. Special thanks go to Jacqui Small, Anne Ryland, David Peters, Penny Stock, Zia Mattocks and Janet Cato.

Fiona Craig-McFeely and Alice Douglas have been superb assistants. Thanks also to Clair Wayman, Jen Gilman (our wonderfully versatile nanny), Lynda Kay and Robert Davies for his expert help in Spain.

Together with energy, humour and enthusiasm, photographer Pia Tryde has produced beautiful and descriptive images. I must also thank Nick Pope and Ian Skelton for the splendid cut-out photography.

Many thanks also to the following people who have so kindly let me photograph in their gardens: John and Colleen Matheson; The Manor Gardening Society; Nancy McCabe; Dean Riddle; David and Carolyn Fuest; Humphrey and Isabelle Bowden; Nick and Hermione Tudor; Vanessa de Lisle; Karl and Pia Sandeman; Lisa Bynon and Mona Nehrenberg; Timothy Leese and Robert Chance. Special thanks to my New York friend, Tricia Foley, for her help, guidance and hospitality, and to Ellen O'Neill, who very generously let me invade her Long Island home once more.

Big hugs for Alastair, Tom, Georgia, Grace and my parents, John and Jean, who, once again, put up with me and the agonies and angst of creating a book.